KNOWING YOUR RIGHTS AND USING THE COURTS

Second Edition
Amanda Howlett

Straightforward Publishing
www.straightforwardco.co.uk

Straightforward Publishing
Brighton BN2 4EG

ISBN 1847160 71 9
ISBN 13: 9781847160713

Cover design by Bookworks Islington

Printed in England by Biddles Limited Kings Lynn Norfolk

CONTENTS

INTRODUCTION

We are all bound by the law and the British legal system. The framework of the law affects us in many ways, directly and indirectly. Right throughout our lives we will need to have a basic knowledge of the law. In this way, we can operate as citizens more effectively and we can also have a greater understanding of our rights and obligations.

The book is not a detailed textbook on the law. The purpose is to outline the law, in enough depth, and ensuring that the reader has understood the law and can then apply that law in a practical way.

This book covers, in the main, the legal system as it operates in England and Wales. To cover Scottish law in the same book would have been too great a task.

An attempt has been made to outline the operation of the legal system and also to describe the players in that system, such as solicitors and barristers and to describe the framework of financial aid that can be accessed through the legal help scheme. There is a detailed chapter on putting together a small claim and going to court with that claim. For many people, the small claims court is the most common method of seeking redress against an individual or company.

The chapters that follow the small claims court cover accidents and compensation, law and the consumer, employment law, the legal relationship between children and adults, financial provisions for children, divorce, Civil Partnerships, bereavement and the law, producing a will, the law and neighbours, landlord and tenant and, finally, the law and the police, what to do if you are arrested and how to complain.

The more complicated our society becomes, the more it becomes controlled by laws and regulations, the more that the individual needs to know to be able to be effective. This book cannot hope to be totally comprehensive but does cover as many key areas as possible.

1

HOW THE LEGAL SYSTEM WORKS IN BRITAIN

Legal terms explained

There is a glossary of terms at the back of this book which deals with commonly used legal jargon. However, it is useful to highlight the most common terms right at the outset, as they will be used frequently throughout the book:

Claimant – when legal proceedings are brought, the person or persons, or organisation, bringing the case is called the claimant.

Defendant – The individual or organisation being sued, and therefore defending, is called the defendant.

Solicitor – a solicitor is the lawyer you will see for legal advice relating to your case. This person will have undertaken many years of study and passed all the necessary legal examinations. We will be discussing solicitors in more depth a little later.

Barrister – A Barrister is a lawyer who is a specialist in what is known as advocacy, i.e. speaking in court. A Barrister will have been called to the bar by one of the Inns of Court and passed the barristers' professional examinations. A solicitor will instruct a barrister to represent you in court proceedings. However, barristers will not normally be the persons giving individuals legal advice in the first instance. The legal profession is, basically, split into two, barristers and solicitors, both of whom are lawyers.

Writ – A judicial writ is issued to bring legal proceedings. Civil cases are started in the courts by issuing and serving a writ. This document is completed either by an individual bringing the case or by a solicitor on behalf of the individual. It is issued by the court.

Litigant in person – a litigant is someone who is bringing legal proceedings or suing. A litigant-in-person is someone who chooses to represent themselves in court, without a lawyer.

Damages – Civil claims in the courts are for damages, which is money claimed from the defendant to compensate the claimant for loss arising from the action of default of the defendant. An example might be the sale of a good that has caused injury to a person and it is alleged that the good was faulty at the time of purchase.

Using the legal system to resolve disputes

If you are contemplating any form of legal action, with or without solicitors, it is necessary to have a basic idea of how the system works. The more that you understand the processes underlying the legal system, the more effective you will be, both as a citizen and as a potential litigant.

The structure of the court system

The court system in the United Kingdom deals, in the main, with civil and criminal cases. They are heard in either the county court (civil cases) and the Magistrates and Crown Courts (criminal cases)

Civil cases are those that typically involve breaches of contract, personal injury claims, divorce cases, bankruptcy hearings, debt problems, some employment cases, landlord and tenant disputes and other consumer disputes, such as faulty goods.

Criminal cases are those such as offences against the person, theft, damage to property, murder and fraud. These cases, if of a non-serious nature, are heard in the magistrate's courts. If of a serious nature, then they will be heard in the Crown Court and tried by jury.

Criminal cases

The more serious criminal cases are tried on the basis of a document called the *indictment*. The defendant is indicted on criminal charges specified in the indictment by the prosecutor. In most cases, the prosecution is on behalf of the Crown (State) and is handled by an official agency called the Crown Prosecution Service, which takes the case over from the police who have already investigated most of the evidence. The first stage will be to decide whether there is a case to answer. This process, called committal, will be dealt with by a magistrate on the basis of evidence disclosed in papers provided by the prosecutor. If the case proceeds, it is heard in the Crown Court. There are about 70 Branches of the Crown Court in the United Kingdom. The trial is before a judge and jury. The judge presides over the trial and considers legal issues. The jury will decide on the facts (who is telling the truth) and applies the law to those facts. In criminal cases, the prosecution has to prove, beyond reasonable doubt, that the defendant is guilty. The defendant does not have to prove innocence. However, it is the jury who will observe the prosecutor and defending lawyer and decide the case.

In less serious criminal cases (which comprise over 90% of criminal cases) the case is sent for summary and trial in one of over 400 *magistrates* courts. A summary trial means that there is no committal or jury. The case is decided by a bench of magistrates. In most cases there are three magistrates who are lay (unqualified) persons but are from the local community. However, there are now an increasing number of 'stipendiary' magistrates, paid magistrates who are qualified lawyers. Those defendants in criminal cases who are dissatisfied with verdicts may be able to appeal, as follows:

- from the Magistrates courts there is an appeal to the Crown Court on matters of fact or law. From the Crown Court, it might be possible to appeal to the Criminal Division of the Court of Appeal on matters of fact or law
- Certain legal disputes arising in the Magistrates court or the Crown Court can be taken before the divisional court of the High Court.

- Matters of important legal dispute arising in the Crown Court can be taken to the House of Lords

Civil cases

The majority of people who buy this book will be taking civil action of one form or another. Increasingly, people are becoming litigants-in-person as this enables people to access the courts and obtain justice without incurring high costs. The only real costs are the court fees and other incidental costs such as taking time off work and so on.

The county court

The county court deals with civil cases, which are dealt with by a judge, or a district judge. A case can be started in any county court but can be transferred back to the defendant's local court.

All cases arising from regulated credit agreements must be started in the county court, whatever their value.

County courts deal with a wide range of cases ranging from bankruptcy and family matters to landlord and tenant disputes. The most common cases are:

- Consumer disputes, for example faulty goods or services
- Personal injury claims, caused by negligence, for example traffic accidents, accidents caused by faulty pavements and roads, potholes etc
- Debt problems, for example someone seeking payment
- Some undefended divorce cases and some domestic violence cases
- Race and sex discrimination cases
- Employment problems, usually involving pay.

Small claims in the county court

A case in the county court, if it is defended, is dealt with in one of three ways. These ways are called 'tracks' The court will, when considering a case, decide which procedure to apply and allocate the case to one of the following tracks:

- The small claims track

- The fast track
- The multi-track

The small claims track is the most commonly used and is the track for claims of £5000 or less. Overall, the procedure in the small claims track is simpler than the other tracks and costs are not usually paid by the losing party.

Following a brief summary of the other courts in the United Kingdom, we will be looking in more detail, in chapter 4, at how to commence and process a small claim. In the main, readers of this book will be concerned with the small claims track and it is therefore necessary to outline that process in depth. We will also be looking, in chapter 2, at the legal help scheme. This scheme enables those with a low income to get free legal advice from a solicitor and assistance with preparing a case.

The magistrates' court

As we have seen, magistrate's courts deal with criminal cases in the first instance and also deal with some civil cases.

The cases are heard by Justices of the Peace or by District Judges (magistrates courts). All cases heard in a magistrate's court are from within their own area.

Criminal offences in the magistrate's court

Magistrate's courts deal with criminal offences where the defendant is not entitled to a trial by jury. These are known as 'summary offences' and involve a maximum penalty of six months imprisonment and/or a fine up to £5000. Magistrates also deal with offences where the defendant can choose trial by jury. If this is the case, the case is passed up to the Crown Court.

The youth court

The youth court deals with young people who have committed criminal offences, and who are aged between 10-17.

9

The youth court is a part of the magistrate's court and up to three specially trained magistrates hear the case. If a young person is charged with a very serious offence, which in the case of an adult is punishable by 14 years imprisonment or more, the youth court can commit him/her for trial at the Crown Court.

Civil cases in the magistrates' court

As we have seen, the vast majority of civil cases are dealt with in the county courts. However, the magistrate's court can deal with a limited number of cases, as follows:

- Some civil debts, e.g. arrears of income tax, national insurance contributions, council tax and Value added Tax arrears
- Licences, for example, licences for clubs and pubs
- Some matrimonial problems, e.g. maintenance payments and removing a spouse from the matrimonial home
- Welfare of children, e.g. local authority care orders or supervision orders, adoption proceedings and residence orders

The Crown Court

The more serious criminal cases are tried in the Crown Court. The following are dealt with:

- Serious criminal offences to be heard by judge and jury
- Appeals from the magistrates court-which are dealt with by a judge and at least two magistrates
- Someone convicted in the magistrates court may be referred to the Crown Court for sentencing.

The High Court

The High Court will hear appeals in criminal cases and will also deal with certain civil cases. The High Court also has the legal power to review the actions or activities of individuals and organisations to make sure that they are both operating within the law and also are acting justly. The High Court consists of three divisions, as follows:

10

The Family Division

The Family Division of the High Court will deal with more complex defended divorce cases, wardship, adoption, domestic violence and other cases. It will also deal with appeals from the magistrates and county courts in matrimonial cases.

The Queens Bench Division

The Queens Bench Division of the High Court will deal with larger claims for compensation, and also more complex cases for compensation. A limited number of appeals from county and magistrates courts are also dealt with. The Queens Bench Division can also review the actions of individuals or organisations and hear libel and slander cases.

The Chancery Division

The Chancery Division deals with trusts, contested wills, winding up companies, bankruptcy, mortgages, charities, and contested revenue such as income tax.

The Court of Appeal

The Court of Appeal deals with civil and criminal appeals. Civil appeals from the high and county courts are heard, as well as from the Employment Appeals Tribunal and the Lands Tribunal. Criminal Appeals include appeals against convictions in the Crown Courts, and points of law referred by the Attorney General following acquittal in the Crown Court or where a sentence imposed is seen as too lenient.

The House of Lords

The House of Lords deals mostly with appeals from the Court of Appeal, where the case involves a point of law of public importance. Appeals are mostly about civil cases although the Lords do deal with some criminal appeals. If there is dissatisfaction with a finding of the House of Lords then the claimant can take a case higher through the European Court System.

The court of First Instance

The Court of First Instance is based in Luxembourg. A case can be taken to this court if European Community law has not been implemented properly by a national government or there is confusion over its interpretation or it has been ignored. A case which is lost in the Court of First Instance may be taken to appeal to the European Court of Justice.

The European Court of Justice of the European Communities

The European Court of Justice advises on interpretation of European Community law and takes action against infringements. It examines whether the actions of those members of the European Community are valid and clarifies European Community law by making preliminary rulings. It also hears appeals against decisions made by the Court of First Instance.

The European Court of Human Rights

The European Court of Human Rights deals with cases in which a person thinks that their human rights have been contravened and for which there is no legal remedy within the national legal system.

2

USING SOLICITORS AND BARRISTERS – THE LEGAL HELP SCHEME AND OTHER SOURCES OF ADVICE

For those contemplating taking legal action, there are a number of options. The first option is usually to visit a solicitor to gain legal help and to launch your case. However, it is a fact that many people are put off going to see a solicitor because of the costs involved. In many cases, unfortunately, this results in people being denied justice.

As we have seen, the costs of launching a civil case in the county court are minimal and the process is relatively straightforward. Chapter 4 deals with this process in depth. However, many people would still rather work with the help and guidance of a solicitor. This chapter outlines the work of solicitors, the other forms of legal advice available and also outlines the legal help scheme for those on low income.

Solicitors

Solicitors are trained to deal with a large range of legal problems. Large firms tend to be formed as partnerships and will have specialist solicitors working in defined areas, such as crime, family, landlord and tenant and so on. Solicitors are heavily regulated by the Law society and must have no personal interest in the matter in dispute. Solicitors must take out compulsory indemnity insurance to indemnify them against negligence and the profession also runs a 'compensation' fund to compensate those who have suffered loss at the hands of unscrupulous solicitors.

Solicitors do not come cheap and will charge by the hour, charges being anything up to £90 per hour. There are often fixed fees for matters such as conveyancing.

For advice which they consider they may need a second opinion, solicitors will usually seek 'counsels advice' which is given by a barrister.

A Barrister is a specialist in advocacy, operating from 'chambers' and costing anything up to £300 per hour. Often, high profile cases, such as tax evasion and libel and slander, will be conducted by barristers.

Anyone considering launching legal action will need to consider whether or not they wish to use a solicitor. For simple small claims, it is not necessary to use a solicitor as the process is designed to assist the layperson. However, the following instances may demand that you use a solicitor:

- Moving house
- Getting divorced
- Getting arrested
- Other complex legal maters, such as negligence and nuisance compensation claims

Never use a solicitor without first obtaining an estimate of their likely charges in the matter. Some solicitors will attempt to be vague over such matters but it is highly desirable for you to be assertive on the matters of cost estimates. Ensure that the estimate is in writing and is broken down and clear. Most solicitors now issue a 'client engagement' letter to their clients as recommended by the Law Society.

Solicitor's charges will principally be based on the amount of time spent on the case, as solicitors usually charge by the hour. The longer it takes, the more it will cost you. If the matter is complex, a solicitor will usually look at the case and decide how much they will do and how much a junior will cover, in order to minimise the costs.

The notion 'the cheapest is best' is not always correct or advisable when dealing with solicitors, as the quality of advice and degree of organisation will vary according to the solicitors used. Usually, larger practices are better able to offer specialist advice and are also better organised and easier to get access to.

Choosing the right firm

The best way to choose a solicitor is by recommendation, for example one that a friend has used. It will be necessary to ensure that the firm that is recommended has the right experience to represent you adequately. In some areas, all solicitors will generally have specialism, such as property conveyancing. However, for obtaining compensation for personal injury, or an employment law dispute then you will need to ensure that a firm of solicitors has this expertise.

Using a solicitor

Solicitors are, generally, very thorough and meticulous. They have to be, given the professional standards and codes that they have to deal with and also because of the need to obtain all the facts. It is important that, in the first instance, you give the solicitor as much clear information as possible. Further ongoing contact by telephone is charged for. Most solicitors will monitor calls carefully and enter these in a log or journal. Time is money, so therefore you should ensure:

- All information is passed on at the beginning
- Do not contact the solicitor too often. Ask for regular progress reports to be sent to you
- Respond to requests for information from the solicitor straight away
- Require an initial estimate and notification when costs reach the level of the estimate

Aim for a friendly, professional and open working relationship with a solicitor as you are both striving towards the same goal, that is to win your case.

Finally, if you search on line then you can access a wide range of solicitors and gain an indication of their specialist areas. A word of caution: you should always be wary of those solicitors who advertise on television. Many will say 'no win no fee'. Although this sounds attractive, the fees if you do win can be very high indeed. If you do intend to use such a firm make sure that you understand the charges at the outset.

In some cases, you may be dissatisfied with a solicitor and will wish to complain or even sue.

If this is the case then contact the Office for the Supervision of Solicitors or the Legal Services Ombudsman (addresses at the back of this book).

Other sources of legal advice

There is no legal requirement to use a solicitor. People do so when they feel that they need advice in the first instance or feel that their case may be too complex. However, there are law centres operating in each local authority area, often offering free advice and specialising in family and community matters, such as health and housing. Citizens Advice Bureau also offer advice and can be found in each area. In addition, the CAB also has on line advice which can be accessed through their web site. Enter www. Citizen's advice and the site will appear. This is very useful and has written advice on a wide range of areas.

Some bodies, such as the consumer association, also offer advice, again either by phone or on line, about a range of issues affecting the consumer. In addition, if you are a member of a trade union you may be able to get free legal advice from this source, Some banks offer free legal advice and it is worthwhile giving your local branch a ring.

Legal aid

Legal aid can be accessed via the 'legal help scheme'. This scheme used to be known as the 'Green Form' scheme but has changed its name and emphasis.

The legal help scheme provides access to free legal advice for people with low incomes. The solicitor or organisation offering this help has to have a contract with the Legal Services Commission to be able to provide assistance.

What does the scheme cover

The Legal Help Scheme covers help from a solicitor including general legal advice and writing letters, negotiating, getting a barristers opinion and preparing a written case for a tribunal. The scheme does not provide for being represented by a solicitor in court (although the *help at court scheme* and *controlled legal representation* scheme might. The solicitor that you are dealing with will give you further advice concerning these schemes.

16

The scheme may also cover the costs of mediation. Mediation is a process of negotiation where the parties are helped by a neutral mediator who will assist them to find a mutually acceptable solution.

Legal problems covered by the scheme

The legal advice scheme will provide advice on general legal problems, including the following areas:

- undefended divorce, maintenance or disputes over children
- Conveyancing necessary to carry out a court order or following a divorce settlement or legal separation
- Contested adoptions
- Preparing for tribunals, for example, unfair dismissal or unified appeal tribunals (benefit appeals)
- Making a will if someone is over 70 or disabled, or is a parent making provision for a disabled child or is a single parent appointing a guardian
- Accident claims – advice, preparing a case for criminal injuries compensation, getting medical reports.

For the case to qualify for the legal help scheme, two criteria must be met:

- Help may be provided only where it is shown there is a benefit to the person
- Help may be provided only if it is shown that it is reasonable for the matter to be funded.

The legal help scheme covers two hours worth of work by a solicitor (three in the case of divorce or judicial separation). The solicitor can apply for extra time to finish the work under the scheme. In addition to these criteria, there may be other criteria applied, depending on the nature of the case.

Financial conditions for the scheme

If a person has disposable capital over £8000, that person will not be eligible for help under the scheme. This limit is for a person with no dependants.

Income

If a person is claiming income support or income based job seekers allowance, that person will be deemed to be within the limits for the scheme. If this is not the case, eligibility will depend on income, currently gross monthly income of over £2530. If a person is receiving working families tax credit or disabled persons tax credit then that person may be eligible for assistance depending on the amount of benefit received. When assessing a person's disposable income, which is income after all expenses, allowances will be made for dependants. If a person's disposable income is below a certain limit then that person will get free legal help. If the disposable income is more than the define limit no help will be given.

Extra costs that the person may have to pay

If a person is awarded property or money as a result of advice under the scheme in a family case, the solicitor's costs may be taken from the amount.

The amount taken will vary. In some cases where it is seen that hardship will result then no costs are taken. It is important to ensure that this is made clear at the outset and you know what the position is.

How to apply

If a person qualifies for the legal help scheme, they need to see a solicitor or organisation with a contract to provide legal help under the scheme. The solicitor will ask the person to fill in an application form at the initial interview. The solicitor will then be able to decide whether the person qualifies.

Help with representation at court

There are three ways you could be helped if you need to be represented in court for a criminal offence. The first is by a representation order which covers representation by a solicitor and, if necessary, by a barrister in criminal cases. To qualify you will need to meet certain financial conditions. You will automatically meet these conditions if under 18 or on benefits.

Advocacy assistance

Advocacy assistance covers the cost of a solicitor preparing your case and initial representation in certain cases. There are no financial conditions for advocacy assistance.

Free advice and representation at the magistrates court

If you didn't get legal advice before your case comes up at the magistrate's court, you can get free legal advice and representation by the court duty solicitor.

For more information about legal aid in criminal cases, you should visit the Legal Services Commission website, where there is a leaflet called A Practical Guide to Criminal Defence Services.

3

SOLVING DISPUTES AND TAKING LEGAL ACTION

If you are in dispute and feel that you need to revert to using the law, before you do so you should try to solve the dispute amicably. You need to establish the facts of the matter and examine whether or not there actually is a dispute at all or whether the problem could be solved without recourse to the law. You also need to look at the dispute in terms of whether or not realistically you are going to win or whether you will be involved in a long and drawn out expensive battle that you are unlikely to win.

You should ask yourself the following questions before committing a case to court:

- Is your case clear cut or does your opponent have a clear argument?
- What do others think about your case? You need to ask someone who is unbiased.
- What is the value of your claim/ Does it justify the time and expense of going to court?
- What are the likely solicitors costs?

Payments into court
If you do go to court, it is worth noting that the defendant can pay a sum into court, representing the amount of money for which the defendant would settle. If the case proceeds and the plaintiff wins less than that sum, then the defendant will not have to pay the plaintiffs costs.

You should always think carefully about accepting a payment into court and should take legal advice.

Timing of court action

Court actions can, by their very nature, be slow and painstaking. However, the timing depends very much on the nature of the dispute. In cases of emergency where an order is needed to prevent someone from doing something this can be made in a matter of hours. These are known as 'injunctions'. Most disputes, however, often take many months to go through the court procedure. So do not expect a quick victory, as the wheels of justice turn at their own pace.

Damages

Damages is the money which is won in compensation from the defendant. The judge in the dispute will make the order as to damages, which normally consists of a sum of money necessary to place the claimant in the same position as he or she was before the incident occurred.

There is an obligation to 'mitigate' loss which means that the claimant should take reasonable care to reduce the loss as much as possible. Damages can be reduced where the claimant is at fault, for example where the claimant has added to the injury suffered by his or her own actions at the time and subsequently.

Damages for criminal injury

In cases where a criminal injury has occurred and compensation cannot be obtained from the perpetrator, you may be able to get compensation from the Criminal Injuries Compensation Authority. The CICA gives out compensation amounting to millions of pounds each year. The address of the Authority is found at the rear of this book.

The eligibility requirements of the programme are that the matter must be reported to police as soon as possible after it has occurred. The matter has to be filed to the CICA within two years. Those who can claim are:

- Victims of crime
- Dependants of homicide victims
- Foreign citizens

21

Procedures

A claimant can obtain an application from CICA, local victim support schemes, Crown Court witness service, local police stations or local citizens advice bureau. The application should be sent to CICA. The authorities initial decision should be made within 12 months, while reviews and hearings can take several months longer. Compensation can be paid as soon as CICA is notified that the claimant accepts the decision.

Benefits and award limits

The maximum award is £500,000.

Compensable costs

- Medical expenses
- Mental Health expenses
- Lost wages for disabled victims
- Lost support for dependants of homicide victims
- Funerals
- Travel
- Rehabilitation for disabled victims
- Pain and suffering
- Bereavement
- Loss of parental services

Emergency awards

Interim payments can be made where a final decision as to the appropriate award is uncertain. For example, where the victim's medical prognosis is unclear.

Funding

The programme is funded by the taxpayer

Appealing against a CICA decision

There is an appeals panel, which will hear appeals against the findings of the CICA. Details can be obtained from the headquarters of CICA.

What to do if you are sued

In addition to deciding to sue someone, you may find yourself in receipt of a summons or writ through the post. The summons or writ will always provide for a written defence, which has to be filed within a time periods clearly outlined on the document. If you do not file the defence then a judgement will be entered against you automatically.

When receiving a writ or summons the following actions should be taken:

- Check to whom the document is addressed. It may be that it should be for someone else. If this is the case forward it on or return to the sender
- If it is for you read it very carefully indeed. With the summons will be a particulars of claim which will outline what the case is against you
- Note any time limits that you have to adhere to

What form of action you should take will very much depend on the nature of the writ or summons. As we discussed, the case will either be civil or criminal. Most people are aware of the basic criminal offences, such as driving offences etc. A small claim against you could be for a variety of actions, such as breach of contract or negligence.

Most criminal offences require attendance at court. Minor criminal offences require attendance at the magistrate's court. Civil offences will require attendance at County Court if you decide to defend. If you admit a claim then the matter can be settled by post.

In criminal offences, the judge will pass sentence. In civil cases, the judge will enter a judgement and decide on a level of compensation relevant to the action.

If the defendant does not pay the money arising from the judgement, then the following remedies are available:

- Send in the bailiffs to seize goods to the value of the claim.

- Attachment of earnings so that the award is taken directly from the persons salary
- Charging orders over the defendants property
- Garnishee orders that can order money to be taken from a bank account.

4

USING THE COUNTY COURT – COMMENCING A SMALL CLAIM

Having looked briefly at the operations of the legal system, it is now necessary to examine the processes involved in commencing a small claim in the county court. Although a claim depends on the subject matter, the majority of people tend to take action in the county court small claims division.

Commencing a claim

A person can start legal action in any court and if the case is defended the court will decide what procedure to use. If the case is a simple one, with a value of £5000 or less, the court will decide that the small claims procedure will be used and will allocate the case to the small claims track. In most cases, the court will not order that costs are paid by the losing party in a small claims case. For this reason, most people do not use a solicitor when making a small claim. It may, however, be possible to get legal help using the legal help scheme.

Types of case dealt with in the Small claims track

When the court is considering whether to allocate the case to a small claims track it will take into account a number of factors, but the main factor is the value of the case.

If the value of a case is £5000 or less it will generally be allocated to the small claims track. However, if it is a personal injury claim, it will be allocated to the small claims track only if the value of the claim for the personal injuries is not more than £1000. If the claimant is a tenant and is claiming against their landlord because repairs are needed to the premises and the cost of the work is £1000 or less, the case will be allocated to the small claims track.

Types of claims in the small claims court

The most common types of small claims are:

- Compensation for faulty goods, for example washing machines or other goods that go wrong
- Compensation for faulty services provided, for example by builders, garages and so on
- Disputes between landlords and tenants, for examples, rent arrears, compensation for not doing repairs
- Wages owed or money in lieu of notice

If a case proves to be too complex then a judge may refer the case to another track for a full hearing, even if below the limit for that track.

Actions before applying to court

As we saw in the previous chapter, before applying to court it is always necessary to try to solve the problem amicably, or as amicably as possible without recourse to legal action. A person who intends to commence a claim should write a 'letter before action' which should set out terms for settlement before applying to court.

For example, if a television is defective, or workmanship on a car is faulty, there is no point applying to court for compensation before contacting the garage or repair shop. Whilst this may seem obvious, there are cases where people do rush in. Always try to settle before launching court action. It will assist in the case if it does go to court.

Which court deals with a small claim

The court action can be started in any court, but the case can be transferred. If the claim is defended and the claim is for a fixed amount, the court will automatically transfer the case to a defendant's local court (if he or she is an individual not a company). In other cases, either party can ask for the case to be transferred.

Commencing a claim

The claimant commences a claim by filling in a claim form, obtainable from local county courts or legal stationers. They can also be obtained from the internet. The government court site is www.Courtservice.gov.uk. All forms can be obtained from this website as can a host of information on all legal topics.

The form is quite straightforward and asks for details of claimant and defendant and how much is owed. The form also asks for the particulars of the claim. The particulars set out full details of the claim. If there is not enough room on the form then a separate piece of paper can be used. The claimant has a right to spend a little more time on the particulars and can send them to the defendant separately, but no later than 14 days after the claim form.

The forms are designed to be user friendly and are accompanied by guidance notes to ensure that no mistakes are made.

The claimant may be entitled to claim interest on the claim and, if so, must give details of the interest claimed in the particulars of claim. In a personal injury claim the particulars of claim must include the claimants date of birth and brief details of the injuries. The claimant must attach a list of any past expenses and losses that they want to claim for and any expenses and losses that they may incur in the future.

Applying for the claim form to be issued

The claimant must ensure that two copies of the claim form reach the court where court action is to commence and a copy should be kept for records. There will be a fee to pay. Currently this depends on the amount of money to be claimed. You should check with your local county court, small claims division, for the current fees.

In some cases, the fee will be waived, for example if the claimant is receiving income support, working families tax credit, disabled persons tax credit or income based job seekers allowance. If none of these benefits are received, but financial hardship would be suffered if a fee was paid, the fee may also be waived.

The court will stamp the claim form and then, in most cases, serve it on the defendant. The court will give the claimant a notice of issue.

Usually the court will serve the claim form by sending it to the defendant by first class post. The claimant will be deemed to have received it on the second day of posting. If the claimant wishes to serve the claim form his or herself then a request should be made and the court will provide the form and other forms that go with it.

If the case is not defended

If the defendant is not defending the case, then he or she may accept that they owe the money. If this is the case then he or she can pay the money directly to the claimant. If the defendant has accepted that they owe the money, but needs time to pay, they can propose an arrangement, for example that the amount owed is paid in instalments or all the money in one lump sum on a specified future date. If the claimant accepts this offer, he or she will have to return a form to the court requesting 'judgement by admission'. If the defendant does not keep to this agreement the claimant can then take enforcement action.

If the claimant does not accept this offer then he or she must give good reason and a court official will decide what a reasonable arrangement will be. The court will send both parties an order for payment. If the claimant is not happy with the order then he or she will have to write to the court giving reasons and sending a copy to the defendant. A judge will then decide what is reasonable for the defendant to pay. If the defendant does not keep to the arrangement, the claimant can take enforcement action.

If the defendant is defending the case

If the case is to be defended, the defendant has to respond to the claim within 14 days of service (this is the second day of posting). If the particulars of claim were served after the claim form the defendant must respond within 14 days of service of particulars of claim. A defence is launched by the defendant sending back the defence form, which was sent with the claim form.

If the defendant does not send a defence back within the time period then the claimant can ask for an order to be made against him or her.

The defendant can send the defence back to the court or can send the acknowledgement of service form sent with the defence form back to court and the defence form back within 14 days of this. This helps if more time is needed.

When the defence is sent to the court the court will send an allocation questionnaire to both the claimant and the defendant. This must be returned to the court no later than the date specified in it. When the claimant returns the allocation form a fee should also be sent although this can be waived on financial grounds. The court will use the information contained within the allocation questionnaire to decide which track to allocate the case to.

When the court has decided to allocate the case to the small claims track, the claimant and defendant will be sent a notice of allocation. This form will tell the parties what they have to do to prepare for the hearing. These instructions are called 'directions'. One example of directions may be that parties are told that they should send all copies of relevant documents to court, documents that they intend to use in court in the case against the other party. These are sent at least 14 days before the case begins.

There are standard directions for a number of common cases, for example, if the claim is to do with a holiday then there will be standard directions from the courts as to the evidence needed.

The day of the hearing

The notice of allocation will usually specify the time, day and date of hearing, where the hearing will take place and how much time has been allowed for it. If the claimant wants to attend the hearing but for some reason cannot, then a letter should be sent to the court requesting a different hearing date. A fee is payable and the court will only agree to this request if it is based on reasonable grounds.

A claimant can also ask the court to deal with a claim in his or her absence, A typical case might be where the costs and time to reach the court are disproportionate. If this is the case then a letter should reach the court at least seven days before the case.

In some cases, the court will not set a final hearing date. The following are alternatives used by the courts:

- The court could propose that the case is dealt with without a hearing. If both parties have no objections then the case can be decided on the papers only. If the parties do not reply by the date given then the court will usually take that silence as consent
- The court may hold a preliminary hearing. This could happen if the claim requires special directions which the judge wants to explain to the parties personally or where the judge feels that the claimant or defendant has no real prospect of succeeding and wants to sort out the claim as soon as possible to save everyone time and expense, or if the papers do not show any reasonable grounds for bringing the claim. A preliminary hearing could become a final hearing where the case is decided.

Preparing a case

It is important that a case is prepared carefully – the court has to be convinced. A reasonable amount of time should be spent ensuring that all the facts are entered, all dates specified and all paperwork is available. The following points are a general guide to what preparation should be made:

- someone with low income can use the legal help scheme to cover the costs of legal advice, but not representation from a solicitor. This advice can be extremely useful and can include getting expert reports, for example on faulty goods. However, a report can only be used in court with permission of the court
- notes about the case should be set out in date order. This will help you to present your case and will make sense to a judge. All backing documentation should
- be taken to court and be presented if asked for. This documentation should be organised around the presentation, in chronological order
- damaged or faulty goods should be taken as evidence. If it is not possible to do this then photographs should be taken instead

- evidence of expenses should be taken along and any receipts kept
- all letters about the case should be taken to court
- in most cases, the claimant and defendant may be the only witnesses. If the court has agreed that other witnesses can attend, then they must attend. If a witness has difficulty getting time off work then a witness summons can be served. The courts will explain how to do this.

The final hearing

The final hearing is usually held in public but can be held in private if the parties agree or the judge thinks that it is necessary. Hearings in the small claims track are informal and the usual rules of evidence do not apply. The judge can adopt any method of dealing with the hearing that he or she thinks fit and can also ask questions of the witnesses before anyone else. A lay representative has the right to speak on behalf of a person at a hearing but only if that party attends the hearing.

If an interpreter is needed, because English is not the first language then an experienced advisor should be consulted, or the court may be able to advise on this.

At the end of the hearing the judge will pass judgement. The judge has to give reasons for the decision that he or she has arrived at. If the claimant wins, he or she will get the court fee back as well as the sum awarded. If the claimant loses no fees will be returned. However, it is unlikely that any other costs will have to be paid.

Appealing against a decision

A party may appeal against a judgement in the small claims track only if the court made a mistake in law or there was a serious irregularity in the proceedings. If a person wishes to appeal then a notice of appeal must be filed within 14 days. A fee is payable although this can be waived in cases of financial hardship. If you do wish to appeal a decision, it is very likely that you would need to consult a solicitor or an experienced advisor to help you.

Enforcement of orders

If a defendant does not pay, the claimant can go back to court and enforce that order. As we have seen, there are a number of remedies, such as bailiff, attachment of earnings and garnishee order. Another fee is involved when enforcing. The court will give you full details of different remedies and fees involved.

5
ACCIDENTS AND COMPENSATION

This chapter deals with accidents to a person and the position following that accident. If you hurt or damage yourself or your property through your own negligence, there will be no one to claim from except yourself. However, if a person is injured as a result of the negligence of someone else, there may be a claim for damages against that person.

The general rule covering claiming damages against another is that you can claim damages if:

- You have been injured against someone else's failure to take precautions against causing possible injury to another or their possessions
- It was a situation where a reasonable person would have been aware of the risk of your being injured and
- He or she would have taken precautions to avoid the risk.

What to do after an accident has occurred
The main point is that if you think that you may be able to lodge a claim for compensation following an accident then you should act very quickly. Often, after an accident, a person may be too shaken or upset to act quickly. A person causing damage to another quite often knows that this is the case and will seize the advantage.

The following are the steps that should be followed:

- Make sure that you have the name and address of all witnesses to the accident and that the police are called. Make sure that, if Injuries are involved, these are examined by a doctor or hospital.

- Make sure you have accurate records. Make sure that you have detailed, photographic or sketched evidence relating to the actual scene of the accident. Write out a full description and inform your insurers

When can a person sue?
To prove negligence, a person must show the following:
- It was reasonably foreseeable that harm would result from a failure to take care
- There was a duty of care owed to another and that duty was not discharged
- Damage or injury to persons or property from the failure to take reasonable care

Even if a person can establish all of the above, the person at fault may still be able to provide a defence, explained further on.

Time limits in which a person must claim for negligent acts
The law lays down time limits within which an individual must take legal proceedings in relation to negligence. In cases of personal injuries or death, there is a three year time limit, which runs from the date of the injury or when the individual knew of the injury. One of the important points here is that a person can claim from the date that they knew of the injury. So an injury, say from asbestosis, may have started to form many years ago, and over a period of years. However, the claim only has to be made within three years of knowing about the injury.

Children can bring a claim for personal injury in their own right within three years of their 18th birthday, Children under 18 years must sue through their parent or guardian on their behalf.

Civil and criminal proceedings
The main aim of criminal proceedings against another is to allocate blame and punish the wrongdoer. The aim of civil proceedings is to compensate a person for that wrongdoing. However, it is true that criminal courts can also order compensation in cases of negligence.

Alternative sources of compensation

Because the law imposes limitations on the time taken to claim and also because there is cost and expense involved in taking a case to court, many people wisely take out insurance. To take care of ourselves, we take out life policies, personal accident insurance, health policies, household and all risk policies and so on. To take care of other people we take out liability insurance. This means in case of accidents, there is a form of insurance that can compensate. Quite often, the only loss suffered by the person causing negligence is emotional. The consequences of what has happened stay with him or her for a long time, depending on the nature of the accident.

Defences to a claim of negligence

Even f it has been established that another person was legally at fault in causing you harm, he or she may have a successful defence to your claim. This can reduce or eliminate your chances of winning negligence cases.

The most common defences are:
- Contributory negligence
- Voluntary assumption of risk
- Unavoidable accident

Only one of the above defences need apply.

Contributory negligence

It can be argued that the victim has contributed to the accident by acting in a way that exacerbated the problem. A classic case is where, if you have an accident with another vehicle and that vehicle was driving with no headlights, the fact that you are driving with dipped headlights means that you have contributed to the subsequent damage by not ensuring that other vehicles can be fully seen.

Voluntary assumption of risk

If you agree to run a risk, and an accident does occur then you may not be able to claim against another.

This could happen, for example, where you accept a lift from someone who you know is drunk and there is subsequently a crash. You knew of the risk and therefore you will limit your claim for damages.

However, those who put up notices that try to absolve them against risk will find that they are invalid in law. Such notices may be in a car wash or shop and say something to the effect that accidents are not the liability of the owners. In this case, a risk is not being taken by you.

Unavoidable accidents

When an accident occurs because of something or some situation which could not have been foreseen and against which precautions could not have been taken, this undermines any claim for compensation. An example is where a traffic accident took place because of a sudden illness, which is not contributed to negligence.

The occupier's liability

Whether you can sue someone for an accident occurring in the home really depends on the nature of the accident. Accidents occur in the home for many reasons and it really depends on the cause and effect principle.

The fundamental rule when looking at accidents in the home is that the occupier, or person with legal responsibility for the premises, must exercise a reasonable degree of care to ensure that their premises are reasonably safe for others to use. The occupier may not only be a householder. The occupier is anyone with legal responsibility for any premises, be they swimming baths, libraries or residential property.

Only people who suffer physical injury or damage to property can claim. The occupier can be liable if the injury is caused indirectly by the dangerous state of the premises. The occupier's primary responsibility is to anyone who visits the premises as a guest, to do a job, or for some other lawful purpose, such as to carry out a repair. The liability for harm suffered on property also extends to people that you do not invite, such as authorised walkers. Ramblers, children tempted by some attraction, such as a pond or apple tree, trespassers and undesirables. The extent of your duty and responsibility will diminish with each category.

Accidents in the street

The classic is where someone falls over on the highway or outside a railway station. You may hurt yourself or damage your belongings. If you do fall because of a loose or uneven paving slab, or fall into a pothole then the highways authority may be to blame.

Defining 'highway'

A highway comprises the road that you will cross (carriageway) and the footpath. Local highway authorities are:

- County councils
- Metropolitan borough councils outside London
- London Borough councils
- District councils or parish councils for unclassified roads, footpaths and bridleways

Motorways and trunk roads are responsibilities of the DETR (Department of Environment, Transport and Regions). All of these authorities maintain highways at public expense and are responsible to those who use them. If the accident was caused by a mains cover or ongoing maintenance and repair, the appropriate organisation to claim from may be the utility company, such as British Telecom.

When a local authority may be liable

The authority is only responsible for dangers arising from the condition of the highway. Not all accidents in streets are attributable to this. The liability of the highway authority is based on lack of due care. If the authority could not have know of the danger then it will have a defence.

The local authorities responsibility will also extend to lighting, objects in the street that could cause damage, and also failing to provide adequate warnings in any other situation that could lead to harm.

Accidents at work

Liability for the safety of the workforce is regulated by a fairly in depth framework of law.

This includes Health and Safety law and also the law governing negligence. Obviously, in a workplace there is a greater risk to the individual, in particular depending on the nature and type of work undertaken. If you are an employer, it is your legal responsibility to assess what potential harm your employers or others might face in the workplace. There is a requirement to decide on the necessary safety conditions and make sure that they are implemented. There are many heavy penalties facing employers who do not comply with legislation and general tests of reasonableness, from being closed down to being taking to an industrial tribunal.

Employers liability insurance
By law, employers must take out insurance to cover themselves against any claims for compensation from the employee. In addition, a public liability policy is taken out to cover the employer against any claims from other parties as a result of negligence.

Insurers will inspect a business where there are known risks, such as a chemical factory and insist on compliance with standards, Failure to do so will nullify the policy.

Health and safety legislation
The Health and Safety at Work Act 1974 imposes a general duty on employers to ensure, so far as is reasonably possible, the health, safety and welfare at work of all employees.

There are many regulations within the Act, which cover many specific types of business. So, in addition to the fundamental basic requirements that cover all workplaces, there are heavier regulations depending on the nature of the business.

Contributory negligence
Employees have a duty to co-operate with the employer to take care for their own and others safety. Employees who put their colleagues or members of the public at risk by carelessness or by disobeying safety instructions can also be deemed to be negligent and also liable for damages against another.

Staff at risk from the public

Employers can be held liable if they fail to take all reasonable steps to prevent and guard against the likelihood of risk to their employees. There are certain categories of people who are at risk more than others, such as benefits workers, nurses and so on. Any claim for compensation is usually in tandem with criminal action. Employees who are victims of criminal assault can also claim from the Criminal Injuries Compensation Board.

Medical accidents

In the same way as others who are bound by the general rules of negligence, doctors and dentists have to exercise a reasonable degree of skill so as not to cause foreseeable injury to their patients.

It is important to realise that medical accidents do occur without anyone to blame. A simple routine operation can go wrong because of the reaction of the patient. Compensation cannot be recovered in these cases because no one can say that any particular doctor or hospital is in the wrong.
In all cases, liability is based on lack of due care. In some cases, this is beyond argument. In others, not so clear-cut.

Establishing cause and effect

It can be very difficult to establish cause and effect. Doctors are often loath to testify against fellow professionals in negligence suits, patients have to prove that the doctor failed to practice an acceptable standard of professional skill which is not easy for a lay person to establish or judge. In addition, courts tend to be more protective of doctors for fears of opening the floodgates to litigation. A victim of medical negligence, or accident has the additional problem of establishing that it was the doctors or hospitals negligence which resulted in the injury. This is a particular problem where the negligent conduct is said to be a *failure* to treat or to diagnose.

If you think that you may have a claim for medical negligence you will need to take legal advice to be able to further the claim. There are many legal practices who specialise in medical negligence and they will be able to tell you whether you can claim.

Defences to negligence

The doctors negligence may be based on failing to provide information to the patient or in failing to obtain the patients consent to treatment. In the case of a treatment that carries some risk, and information is given, then the doctors negligence is reduced in the case of accident. If no information was given, the patient will be able to sue.

If no consent at all has been given to a doctor to adopt a particular procedure the doctor is particularly liable.

Doctors have also been held to be liable for:

- Failing to investigate the patients medical history before administering further treatment
- Failing to provide adequate information so that those responsible for subsequent treatment are duly informed

Who is responsible?
NHS Treatment

For NHS treatment the health authority or self-governing hospital trust is responsible for any proven lapses in skill or care of its employees. It will not matter whose fault or error caused the accident.

In the case of a fee-paying patient, the doctor must be sued personally. If the injury was caused by negligent nursing care the private hospital is sued. All doctors carry insurance under special schemes.

General non-medical safety in hospitals

Security is a growing problem in hospitals. Numbers of people wander in and out of hospital premises for many reasons. However, there have been some horrific cases of injuries to patients in hospitals from outsiders. Again, the hospital is liable for a patient's safety.

Making a complaint

There is a complaints procedure for any person, patient or not, who wishes to lodge a complaint against a specific hospital or member of staff.

This does not however, cover financial compensation. If financial compensation is being sought then legal action must be taken.

To use the complaints procedure a person must be a patient or former patient of the practitioner or institution concerned. It is possible to complain on behalf of existing or former patients but the hospital or practice must agree that the person complaining is a suitable representative.

A complaint must be made as soon as possible after the incident. The time limit for complaints is usually six months form the date of the incident. However, if a hospital or practice is unaware of there being any cause for complaint, the six-month time limit begins from when they first became aware. This start date must be within twelve months of the date of the incident.

There is discretion to waive the limit where it would be unreasonable to expect the complaint to have been made in time, for example, because of grief or trauma. It must, however, still be possible to investigate the complaint.

There are three stages in the complaints procedure:

- Local resolution
- Independent revue panel
- The Health Service Ombudsman

Local resolution
If a person wishes to make a complaint about any aspect of NHS treatment they have received or been refused, they should first go to the practice, hospital or trust concerned and ask for a copy of their complaints procedure.

Independent review panel
If local resolution fails to solve the matter then the matter should be referred to the trust or, in the case of a family practitioner, the local health authority or primary care trust for an independent review.

The matter is then referred to a convenor who has a number of options in deciding how to proceed with a complaint:

They can:

- Refer the complaint back to the practice where the complaint began for further action under local resolution
- Arrange for both parties to attend conciliation
- Set up an independent review panel which will investigate the complaint
- Take no further action if it is felt that everything has been done that could be done

If the person is still unhappy then the matter can be referred to the Health Service Ombudsman. There are three Ombudsman, one each for England, Wales and Scotland. The addresses of the Ombudsman can be obtained from any hospital or medical practice. The Ombudsman has far reaching powers at the highest levels and will investigate the complaint, set time limits and advise you accordingly. The decision of the Ombudsman is final.

6

THE LAW AND THE CONSUMER

In the previous chapters, we looked at how the legal system works and how to make a small claim, plus how to deal with the matter of accidents and compensation. We will now to look at the different areas of law as it affects people in their every day lives. If you feel that you have a grievance against another, and that this grievance could eventually be taken to court, then it is absolutely necessary to understand the area of law that can be used to take the case to court.

This chapter deals with the area of consumer law. A large percentage of cases that reach the small claims court are those that have arisen out of transactions between the consumer and a provider. These transactions can be between a holidaymaker and the travel company, a customer and a shop or a car owner and a garage. The list is long. One factor unites all consumers however, and that is that there is a strong body of law governing the relationship between buyer and seller.

Buying Goods

The law

When you choose to buy goods from a trader, such as a shop, market stall etc, you enter into a contract that is governed by the Sale of Goods Act 1979 (amended by the Sale and Supply of Gods Act 1994). This law gives you certain automatic statutory rights.

A contract is a legally binding agreement between two or more parties involving the exchange of something of value, i.e. money for goods. A lot of contracts are verbal. These are still contracts. What governs the contract is the intention of the parties to that contract.

A recent change in the law has introduced the concept of 'third parties' to contracts. This means that if you give a gift to someone, they can have rights under the contract as a third party.

If possible, it is important to inform the retailer at the time of purchase that the good is going to be given as a gift.

A contract has to contain certain important elements to be binding. The most important three are:

- The offer – something is on offer and you wish to buy it
- Acceptance – the shop agrees to sell it to you at an agreed price
- Consideration – the legal term for payment in exchange for the goods.

As well as the implied rights laid down in the Sale of Goods Act 1979, discussed above, you can also have 'express rights' in a contract. These are where you negotiate special terms important to your contract, for example, a particular specification or a particular deliver date.

Statutory rights
The Sale of Goods Act 1979, as amended, states that goods should be:

- of a satisfactory quality, i.e. of a standard that a reasonable person would consider to be satisfactory – generally free from fault or defect, as well as being fit for the purpose for which they are intended, of a reasonable appearance and finish, and safe and durable.
- As well as being fit for the purpose for which they are generally sold, goods should also be fit for any specific or particular purpose made known at the time of the agreement
- As described – goods should correspond to any description applied to them. This could be verbally, words or pictures on a sign, packaging or in an advert.

Unfair Contract Terms 1977 and the Unfair Terms in Consumer Contracts Regulations 1977
Between them, these laws allow you to challenge any contractual term that may be unfair or unreasonable, unfairly weighted against you, or ambiguous.

Standard contract terms should be written in clear understandable language. It is illegal to have a contractual term that restricts your contractual rights, or avoids any liability for death or personal injury.

Misrepresentation Act 1967

If you have been told something factual about goods that made you decide to buy them, that turns out to be untrue, then they have been misrepresented to you. In most case's, you can back away from the deal and have your money back. This can be a complex area of law involving different types of representation and different legal remedies. If you feel that you have been misrepresented then you should take advice before pursuing the matter to court.

Trade Descriptions Act 1968

Sometimes, if a trader makes a misrepresentation about goods, a criminal offence may be committed under this Act. For example, a market trader tells you that a jacket he is selling is 100% leather. You buy it, on the basis of this information and discover that it is 45% leather and 55% other. The goods were mis-described to you and you can ask for your money back.

Misleading Price Regulations

The law does not control a price that the trader can charge for goods. However, you are entitled to expect the price of a good or goods to be displayed clearly so that you understand the full cost. If goods are incorrectly priced, you cannot force a trader to supply them to you.

Faulty goods

If you have been sold a faulty good, the first thing to do is to act promptly. You should inform the trader about any problems, either in person or in writing. You should stop using the goods. It is the trader's responsibility to arrange to collect faulty goods that you have rejected, especially if the items are large. With smaller items it may be more practical to take them back yourself.

The law states that you must be give a 'reasonable' amount of time to examine goods and check that they are satisfactory. If they are not, and you have acted promptly, you will be entitled to a refund.

What is a reasonable time will depend on individual circumstances – you would probably have less time to check a toaster than a car – but recent case law suggests a week or so.

If you leave it too long then you may only be entitled to reasonable compensation. Usually, this means repair or replacement, or if this is not possible or acceptable, then reasonable compensation. The amount depends on how long you had the goods, the nature or degree of the problem and how much use you have had from them.

If you buy goods that turn out to be faulty, and you decide to allow the trader to repair them, you will not have lost any of your rights to have your money back later if the repair is unsuccessful. If the trader offers to replace faulty goods, then get an agreement in writing that, if the replacements are faulty also, you will still be able to reclaim your money. This is called 'reserving your rights'

If you have paid for the goods by credit card (not debit or charge card) and the value of each item is £100 or more, then the credit card company has obligations to you too. These rights are given to you under the Consumer Credit Act 1974, under a principle known as 'Equal Liability'. This means that the credit card company and the supplier have the same obligations and responsibilities to you for the goods being satisfactory. You can complain to both the supplier and the credit card company.

Private Sales
When you buy goods from a private individual, you do not have the same rights as when buying from a trader. The legal principle of 'Caveat Emptor' or 'Buyer Beware' operates. You have no rights to expect goods to be of a satisfactory quality or fit for their purpose, so you should check goods thoroughly before you buy them. However, the law does say that even private sellers should not misrepresent goods to you. Again, the Misdescriptions Act applies.

Second Hand Goods

You have full rights under the Sale of Goods Act when you buy second hand goods, although the law does say that you must consider the price paid, and if necessary be prepared to lower your expectations about their performance – for example it would not be reasonable to expect a ten year old, high mileage car to give you the same or a similar performance as a brand new car.

Sale of Goods

You have full rights under the Sale of Goods Act when purchasing sale goods. However, if the goods were reduced in price because of a defect, that was either brought to your attention at the time or should have been obvious to you at the time of examination, then you would not be able to have your money back later for that particular fault.

Typical problems when purchasing goods

The following are common scenarios and common answers to problems:

- It isn't our fault that the goods are defective – you should go back to the manufacturer. Not true, you bought the goods from the trader and the trader is liable for breach of contract, unless he was acting as the manufacturers agent.

- You only have rights for 30 days after purchase. Not true, depending on circumstances, you might be too late to have all your money back by this time, but the trader will still be liable for any breaches of contract, such as the goods being faulty. In fact, the trader could be liable for compensation for up to six years, under the statute of limitations. This places a ceiling on claiming for defective goods or debt generally.

- You must produce your receipt. This is not true. In fact, the trader does not have to give you a receipt in the first place so it would be unfair to want some proof of purchase.

- No refunds can be given on sale items. It depends on why you meant to return them. The Sale of Goods Act still applies, but you will not be entitled to anything if you knew of any faults before purchase, or if the fault has been obvious to you. Also, you are not entitled to anything if you simply change your mind.

- We do not give refunds at all – you must accept a credit note. Again, it depends on why you want to return the goods. If you have changed your mind then the shop does not have to do anything. However, if the goods are faulty, incorrectly described or not fit for their purpose, then you are entitled to your money back (provided you act quickly) and you do not have to take a credit note.

When are you not entitled to anything?

- If you were told of any faults before you bought the goods
- If the fault was obvious and it would have been reasonable to have noticed it on examination before buying
- If you caused any damage yourself
- If you made a mistake, i.e. you do not like the colour, or it is the wrong size etc.
- You have changed your mind about the goods or seen them cheaper elsewhere
- You bought the goods more than six years ago.

Remember, you are bound by contract whenever you buy anything. You should always understand the contract, never rush in or be pressured.

Your rights when buying on credit

When you purchase goods with a credit card or with a credit agreement that a trader has arranged that gives you finance, with a separate finance company, and the total cost of the transaction is more than £100, you will have an equal claim against the finance company. This applies though you may only have paid the deposit by credit. These rights are provided by section 6 of the Consumer Credit Act 1974. You should be careful and beware when you buy under a credit agreement, the finance company can repossess if you do not keep up payments.

Types of credit

Credit cards

As credit cards are easy to use and universally accepted they are the most commonly used form of credit. Under the provisions of section 75 of the Consumer credit Act 1974, if you buy goods or services costing in excess of £100 using a credit card, should the goods or services prove to be defective, you will have an equal claim for compensation against both the seller of the goods and the finance company.

Section 75 (equal liability) only applies to credit transactions, therefore the finance company does not have any liability for purchases that have been paid for by charge cards, as these are debit cards and not credit cards.

Credit sale

These are agreements where the goods are supplied by the trader who, acting as an agent, then arranges finance for the consumer with a separate finance company. A copy of the signed credit agreement is then retained by the consumer, and another copy is then sent to the finance company. If the finance company approves the loan they will sign it and return a copy to the consumer.

Interest free credit

Many stores now offer the consumer the right to purchase expensive items on credit but do not require the consumer to pay anything for several months. These schemes are also credit sales and therefore, the finance is supplied by a separate finance company.

The consumer has to sign a credit agreement and usually has to agree to make payments by direct debit with the option to settle the account in full at the end of the interest free period. If the account is not cleared within the time period, then the finance company will activate the direct debit and payments will be taken out of your account. Interest will also be payable on the total amount of the loan from the date of signing the agreement.

Hire purchase

This type of credit tends to be used for the purchase of vehicles. When the consumer negotiated the purchase of a car from a garage, the garage then sells the car to the finance company, who as the owner, will hire the car to you. You will have the option to buy the car at the end of the agreement. But you will not become the owner until the last payment has been made. any faults that occur will be the responsibility of the finance company, not the garage. You will also need their permission before you sell the vehicle.

Cancellable agreements

Credit agreements signed at the trader's premises are not cancellable. However, if you sign the agreement in your home, you have a short period before the agreement becomes binding and you can cancel without financial penalty.

The benefits of using your credit card

If you buy goods over £100 you have an equal claim over the finance company. This can be very useful if a trader ceases to trade. This benefit also applies if you purchase goods abroad.

You can take either or both parties to the county court. You are entitled to a written statement, which includes the APR before purchasing the goods.

Credit reference agencies

These companies keep records of the credit worthiness of the majority of UK residents and obtain the information from a variety of sources, such as courts. They sell the information to the finance companies who, before they authorise a loan, need to check on your credit history, i.e. whether you have defaulted on a loan.

Buying at Home

When you buy goods in your home, once you have signed an agreement, and then realise that you do not want the goods, you have several options. There are two types of agreement that can be cancellable when they are signed at home, cash and credit. They are covered by different regulations – The Consumer Protection (cancellation of contracts concluded away from business premises) (Amendment) Regulations 1998, and the Consumer Credit Act 1974.

Cash transactions are covered by the Consumer Protection (cancellation of contracts concluded away from business premise (amendment) Regulations 1998.

You should be aware that these regulations do not apply if you have invited a salesman into your home, only in relation to cold calling.

For cash transactions, the regulations give you a period of cooling off of seven days after you sign an agreement, when you are able to cancel without incurring any financial penalty. The cooling off period applies to any cash transaction of over £35, which has been entered into following an unsolicited visit by a salesman. The Regulations apply to the supply of goods and services and also cover agreements for the repair or improvements to property:

The Regulations do not cover agreements for the sale of food or drink, goods supplied by regular rounds-men, such as milk, agreements under £35, agreements relating to land, construction or extension of property, insurance and investment agreements. Catalogue goods that are ordered through an agent are generally exempt from the regulations, provided that the trader already allows the customer to return the goods after seven days.

Finance transactions

When goods are purchased in your home and you sign a finance agreement, the Consumer credit Act 1974 gives you, in most cases, a cooling off period during which you can withdraw from the agreement.

The following agreements are cancellable:

- Agreements that include face to face negotiations with the trader (discussions about the prospective agreement must take place in the presence of the customer)
- Agreements where the finance element is usually arranged by the provider of the goods, as an agent of the finance company

- Agreements that are signed away from the 'trade premises'. These tend to be agreements that you have signed in your home

Agreements that are not cancellable
- Agreements that are signed at the traders premises
- Agreements that you have arranged with your own finance. If the visits were unsolicited, you may still have a cooling off period under the Consumer Protection Regulations 1998.
- Agreements when the negotiations, before the contract is signed, did not take place in the presence of the customer (e.g. discussions over the phone).

Notice of cancellation You must be given a notice of your cancellation rights along with a signed copy of the credit agreement. The finance company will send, by post, a second copy of the agreement, which has been signed by the finance provider, with another notice of your cancellation rights. From the receipt of this copy you have five days in which to cancel the finance agreement and also the 'linked' contract for the supply of goods will also be cancelled at this time.

If the trader does not give you a cancellation notice, then the credit agreement may not be enforceable by the company, without a court order. If you decide to cancel but do not receive a second copy, it is recommended that you write, by recorded delivery, to the finance company, as soon as possible to advise them of your decision.

Guarantees or warranties
A guarantee is most often issued by the manufacture of goods such as electrical goods, or by a company providing services such as replacement windows. It is normally provided free of charge when you buy the good or service. A guarantee usually offers to carry out repairs or make a replacement in the event of a fault arising.

Warranties
A warranty provides the same sort of cover that a guarantee does, but often you have to pay extra for it – for example many electrical stores

provide warranties for five years, at a cost. These sort of warranties are, effectively, insurance policies.

Legal protection with guarantees and warranties

Because guarantees are provided free by manufacturers, the law considers most guarantees to be merely a promise. Unless you bought the goods directly from the manufacturer you will have no claim against them However, most manufacturers will honour guarantees as to not do so would lead to them having a bad name.

The situation is different with a warranty. This is because you will have usually paid for it. This will then change the status of a warranty from a mere promise to do something, into a contractual obligation, which is enforceable in law. If a company does not honour a warranty then they can be sued.

Frequent problems

Fridge freezer purchased 13 months ago and the fridge section has completely failed.
When you buy goods from a shop, you enter into a contract under the Sale of Goods Act 1979 which holds the shop liable for up to six years after purchase, providing that you can demonstrate that the problem is down to an unreasonable fault and not wear and tear. The guarantee issue is not relevant here. That is merely a promise by the manufacturer.
Damp proofing course carried out 5 years ago by a limited company, but noticed rising damp once again. Company claims that it was taken over by new owners and refuses to honour the original 10-year guarantee.
Your contract was with the original company and you cannot enforce the contract or any guarantees. Insurance does exist new for this type of problem

Read any guarantees or warranties carefully – get them in writing!

Buying goods at home- a guide to distance selling regulations

Many people buy goods using the internet or fax, or from home shopping on the TV, or from catalogues. The law recognises that this type of shopping comes with its own type of problems.

For example, what happens if the goods do not turn up or you don't like them once you have received them? People who shop at home now have rights under the Consumer Protection (Distance Selling) Regulations 2000.

Briefly, these Regulations say that you should be given clear information about the order and the company, along with a cooling off period, and protection against credit card fraud and the menace of unsolicited goods.

What isn't covered by these regulations?

- Financial services like banking and insurance
- Auctions
- Goods bought from a vending machine
- Goods bought using a payphone
- Contracts for the sale of land
- Food and drink, or other goods for everyday consumption delivered by rounds men
- Accommodation, transport, catering and leisure facilities for a specific time or date
- Timeshare and package holidays
- The regulations only apply when you buy from a trader who is organised to sell to you without face-to-face contact. So, if you saw something in a shop, went home and bought by phone, this is not distance selling.

The right to clear information

Before you decide to buy, the seller must give you the following information:

- The name of the trader, along with their postal address if you have to pay in advance
- An accurate description of the goods and services
- The price, along with any taxes or delivery charges if relevant and how long the price or offer remains valid
- Delivery arrangements, which should be within 30 days unless agreed otherwise

- Payment arrangements
- The right to cancel the order
- Information about whether you will be liable for the cost of returning the goods if you change your mind
- For services provided over a period of time, such as a mobile phone contract, or a gas supply contract, you must be told what the duration of that contract will be

After you buy, the trader must provide you with the following information:

- Written confirmation of your order (by letter, e-mail or fax) including the information outlined above, if not already provided
- Written information on how to cancel, a contact postal address and details of any guarantees, warranties or after sales service
- Details of how and when to end a contract for the provision of a service if there is no specified finish date
- This information should be sent to you by the time the goods are delivered.

Your right to cancel

The Distance Selling Regulations 2000 give you the right to change your mind and cancel an order within seven working days. If you do decide to cancel, then you should put this in writing, either by letter or you can fax or e-mail. The time limits are:

- For goods – seven working days after the day on which the goods are received
- For services – seven working days after the day on which you agreed to go ahead with the agreement

What isn't covered by this cooling off period?

- Services that are to be provided within seven working days. If you have agreed that the service will be provided before the end of the cooling off period you will not be entitled to cancel once the service has started, but the trader must tell you this in writing.

- Goods made to your personal requirements or specifications
- Goods which may deteriorate quickly, such as flowers or food
- Sealed audio or video recordings or computer software that have been opened.
- Betting, gaming or lottery services
- Newspapers, periodicals or magazines.

7

EMPLOYMENT RIGHTS

There is a strong body of law regulating employers and employees. As we have seen, action against employers can be taken, in certain circumstances, in the county courts. However, in the main, grievances concerning employment are heard at Employment Tribunals.

Employment tribunals are empowered to deal with a wide range of matters arising from a number of legislative provisions, the most important being:

- Complaints of unfair dismissal, applications for redundancy payments,
- references regarding the written particulars of terms of employment,
- complaints regarding suspension from work on medical grounds,
- complaints regarding trade union membership and activities,
- complaints regarding the time off work provisions,
- complaints regarding the right to maternity pay and leave
- complaints under the Sex Discrimination Act 1975,
- complaints regarding time off work for anti natal care ,
- complaints regarding secret ballots on employers premises,
- complaints regarding unreasonable expulsion from trade union membership,
- complaints from trade unions relating to failure of consultation on employment, complaints by trade unions relating to failure to consult them about transfer of undertakings.

The procedure in Employment Tribunals is regulated by the Employment Rights Act 1996. The 2002 Employment Act also introduced significant proposals for change to Employment Tribunals which have been gradually introduced. Rules provide for pre-hearing of assessments of Employment

Tribunal cases at which the tribunal may warn either party to the proceedings that if he wishes to continue an order of costs may be made against him if he loses. The proceedings are intended to be relatively informal both in terms of the pre-tribunal procedure and the hearing. The reasons for the decision of a tribunal must be recorded in a document signed by the chairperson and he must state in this document whether the reasons are recorded in a full or summary form. Full reasons must be recorded in certain types of cases, for example, under the Equal Pay Act, Sex Discrimination Act or the Race Relations Act.

Appeals on questions of law lie in respect of most of the jurisdictions of the Employment tribunals to the Employment Appeal Tribunal, regulated by the Employment Tribunals Act. In respect of most of the kinds of application, which may be made to the Employment tribunals, before there is a hearing, an attempt is made to settle the matter by conciliation using the services of a conciliation officer.

Rights at works

A person's rights at work will depend on his or her statutory rights and the contract of employment. A person's contract of employment should reflect statutory rights and the rights given under the contract cannot take away statutory rights. If a contract states that a person is only entitled to 2 weeks a year holiday and the statutory entitlement is 4, then the contract is invalid. If, however, the contract gives greater rights under the law then the contract will apply.

A persons statutory rights

Statutory rights are legal rights and they arise from laws passed by Parliament. The following areas of law comprise the main statutory areas of law protecting employees. We will be referring to these as we go.

Nearly all workers, regardless of how many hours they work per week, whether full or part time have statutory rights. The rights will differ depending on the nature and circumstances of employment. Sometimes, a worker will gain a right only after that person has been with an employer a certain period of time.

Statutory rights, which all employees have, with the exception of those who are not covered, outlined below, are:

- The right to a written contract of employment within two months of commencing work
- The right to an itemised pay slip. This applies from the day the employee starts work
- The right to be paid at least the national minimum wage.
- The right not to have illegal deductions made from pay
- The right to at least four weeks paid holiday per year, provided the employee has worked for at least 13 weeks
- The right to time off for trade unions and activities. This applies from the date the employee starts work. Time off does not necessarily have to be paid
- Employees have the right to be accompanied by a trade union representative to a disciplinary hearing
- The right to paid time off to look for work if being made redundant. This applies once a person has worked for an employer for two years
- The right to take time off for study or training for 16-17 year olds. This applies from the day of starting work
- The right to be paid for time off for antenatal care. This applies from the day of starting work
- The right to be paid maternity leave and the right to return from this maternity leave. This applies from the date of starting work. If the woman has been with the employer for more than two years, she will be entitled to additional maternity leave, outlined a little further on.
- The right to take unpaid parental leave for men and women, if you have worked for the employer for one year. The right to take reasonable time off to look after dependants in an emergency. This applies from the day of starting work
- The right under health and safety law to work a maximum 48 hour week
- The right under health and safety law to daily and weekly rest breaks

- There are special rules for night workers
- The right not to be discriminated against on the grounds of race, sex or disability
- The right to notice of dismissal, provided the employee has worked for the employer for at least one calendar month
- The right to written reason for dismissal from your employer, provided that you have worked for your employer for at least one year. Women who are pregnant or on maternity leave are entitled to written reasons without having to have worked for any particular length of time
- The right to claim compensation if unfairly dismissed. In most cases, the employee will have had to work for one year to claim unfair dismissal
- The right to claim redundancy pay if made redundant. In most cases, the employee will have had to work for two years to claim redundancy pay
- The right not to suffer the detriment of dismissal for 'blowing the whistle' on a public concern (malpractice) at the workplace. This applies from the day the employee starts work
- The right of a part time employee to the same contractual rights.

Workers not entitled to certain statutory rights
Some worker will not be entitled to some of the above. They are:

- Anyone who is not an actual employee, for example a consultant or freelance worker. Certain rights such as the national minimum wage will apply, as they apply to all, as will health and safety rights and so on
- Employees who normally work outside of the UK
- Members of the police service. However, members of the police service are covered by discrimination law
- Members of the armed forces. They are also covered by discrimination law
- Merchant seamen and share fishermen

- Workers in the transport industry are not entitled to paid holidays or limits on their working hours by law and have to rely on their contract
- Trainee doctors are not entitled to paid holidays or limits on their hours by law and have to rely on their contract.

A worker's rights under their contract of employment

The contract of employment is the legally binding agreement made between the employer and the employee. This can be in writing or be made verbally. Obviously, it is better to have it in writing.

In addition, the contract of employment will also include 'custom and practice' agreements. These are how things are usually done in the workplace, for example, if the employer usually gives one days extra holiday, for whatever reason, this can be included and does not undermine the statutory rights of the employee. If the written contract says one thing, but in practice all employees have been doing something else with the employers knowledge, then custom and practise would form the contract rather than the written statement.

Illegal contracts of employment

Some contracts of employment will be deemed to be illegal if:

- The employee gets all or part of his or her wages as cash in hand and the tax and national insurance contributions are not paid and
- The employee knows that he or she is getting paid like this to avoid tax and national insurance

Right to a written statement of the terms and conditions of employment

All employees, regardless of the number of hours that they work each week, are entitled to a written statement of the main terms and conditions of employment. The statement must give details about:

- Job title
- Wages
- Hours of work

61

- Holiday entitlement
- Sick pay
- Pension scheme
- Notice
- Grievance procedure

Rights to pay

All workers are entitled to be paid for the work that they have done. They are also entitled to be paid if they are ready and willing to work but their employer has not provided them with any work to do. Workers are also entitled to be paid if they are off sick or on holiday, or away from work for a particular reason such as maternity leave, dealing with an emergency at home, jury service and so on. In most of these situations the person will be entitled to be paid. There are however, certain exceptions:

- A woman on maternity leave where her contract gives her less than normal pay. By law, she is entitled to a certain amount of maternity leave, paid, but the law sets out the rate at which she is paid and this may not be as much as her normal daily rate
- A worker on sick pay when that persons contract may less pay than his or her normal pay. Again, the law provides for a statutory minimum.

Right to work in a safe environment

An employer is under a legal duty to make the working environment safe for all employees. This means that the employer must assess what risks there are to health and remedy those risks. Where there is a health and safety risk in the workplace, the employer must take action to eliminate the risk

Time off work

Almost all employees have a statutory right to take time off work with pay for the following reasons:

- To carry out duties as a trade union official

- To carry out duties as a trade union health and safety representative
- To look for work if faced with redundancy
- To receive ante-natal care
- To have a baby
- To study or train for employees aged 16-17

In addition, almost all employees have a right to take time off work, although not necessarily with pay, for the following reasons:

- To participate in Trade union activities
- To perform public duties, for example, justice of the peace or councillor
- To care for their children.
- To attend to unexpected problems with dependants, for example, where child-minding arrangement break down. A dependant includes anyone who reasonably relies on the employee.

Maternity and paternity/Adoption leave
Maternity and Parental pay and leave
Apart from important protection from unfair dismissal because of pregnancy, the Employment Rights Act 1996 provided four further protections in relation to pregnancy - the right to maternity leave, the right to return to work after maternity leave, the right to time off for ante-natal care and the right to maternity pay. The section of the above Act dealing with maternity leave was replaced in its entirety by the Employment Relations Act 1999 Part 1, Schedule 4 which in turn has been amended by the 2002 Employment Act, the provisions of which came into force on April 6th 2003.

Right to maternity leave
The EC Pregnancy Directive (Council Directive 92/85/EEC) regulates maternity leave and is implemented by the 1996 Employment Rights Act.

Also, the 1999 Employment Relations Act as amended by the 2002 Employment Act. The Directive gives all pregnant employees a general right to maternity leave.

Under the 1999 Employment Rights Act, which came into force on the 15th December 1999, the periods of leave were renamed. Maternity leave became ordinary maternity leave (OML) and additional absence became additional maternity leave (AML).

The regulations now clarify that the term remuneration is now limited to 'sums payable by way of wages or salary'. This means, for example, that women will automatically be entitled to retain a company car and a mobile phone and to receive a performance bonus which is not salary.

If a baby is due after 1st April 2007 then there will be the right to 52 weeks maternity leave. This is available to all employees from the first day of employment. The employer must be informed at least 21 days before leave commences that she intends to exercise her rights, and of the date her absence will commence and must be either in writing or oral if the employer requires. The employer can request a certificate of proof of pregnancy and expected date of birth.

If the employee has already a contractual right to maternity pay/leave, she may exercise her right to the more favourable. If there is a redundancy situation during the leave period and it is not practicable because of the redundancy for the employer to continue to employ her under her existing contract, she is entitled to be offered a suitable vacancy before her employment ends. If a woman intends to return to work before the end of maternity leave, 21 days notice must be given. Since women who qualify now have the right to take Additional Maternity Leave, and there is no obligation to notify the employer during the initial notification, then until notification of a return to work is given, the women will retain the right to return but not pay.

Time off for Ante-natal care
To qualify for this right the employee must have made an appointment for ante-natal care on the advice of a doctor, midwife or health visitor. The employer may not refuse time off for the first visit, but for further appointments, the employer may ask for a certificate or appointment card or other evidence.

Statutory Maternity Pay

The Social Security Act of 1996 and the Statutory Maternity Pay regulations of the same year entitle certain employees to statutory maternity pay. This has been amended by the 2002 Employment Act in that there has been an increase in the standard rate of Statutory Maternity pay (SMP) to £117.18 (2008) per week or to 90% of wages if this is lower. (Check current amounts as these are the amounts applicable 2007/2008. If the employee has been working for the employer for 26 weeks by the 15th week before the expected week of confinement, she is entitled to SMP for 18 weeks. She is entitled to nine tenths of her pay for the first six weeks of the 18 and the higher rate of Statutory Sick Pay for the further 18.

To claim SMP, a person must tell their employer, 28 days before maternity leave, that they are pregnant and will be off work because of birth. A medical certificate has to be provided.

When is SMP paid?

How long SMP is paid for depends on when the baby is due. It was paid for up to 26 weeks if the baby was due before April 1st 2007 and for up to 39 weeks if due after this date. The earliest a person can start maternity leave and start getting SMP is 11 weeks before the baby is due. The latest date to start maternity leave and receiving SMP is the week after the week when the baby is born.

If a person is sick with a pregnancy related illness before the baby is due, SMP will start the week following the week that sickness began. If a person is sick with a non-pregnancy related illness they can claim Statutory Sick pay until the week that the baby is due.

Parental leave

The Maternity and Parental Leave Regulations 1999 provide that every person who cares for a young child, or has recently adopted a child, can take time off from work at his or her own convenience to care for that child.

Minimum provisions are set for leave, preconditions are set for leave and the notice that an employee has to give an employer before leave can be taken is set out.

Employers and employees can agree to vary these provisions by using a workforce agreement as long as it is equal to or more favorable than the statutory provisions.

Any employee who has one years continuous employment at the date the leave is due to start, and who has, or expects to have, responsibility for a child at that time can apply to take parental leave. A person will have responsibility for a child under the regulations if he/she has parental responsibility under the Children Act 1989 or is registered as the father under the provision of the Births and Deaths Register Act.

Each employee is entitled to take up to 13 weeks of unpaid parental leave in respect of each child born after, or placed for adoption after, 15th December 1999. In addition, the 2002 Employment Act has widened the scope and range of paternity leave, The Act has introduced the right to two weeks paid leave in addition to the 13 weeks unpaid leave. This became effective from April 2003. Leave must be taken within 8 weeks of the birth of the child or placement of the child through adoption. Statutory Paternity Pay (SPP) will be paid at the rate of either £117.18 per week or 90% of earnings whichever is lower.

For employees to claim paternity leave they must:

- Be employed and have worked for their employer for 41 weeks by the time the baby is due; and
- Be the biological father of the child, or be married to or be the partner of the baby's mother (this includes same sex partners, whether or not they are registered civil partners); and
- Have some responsibility for the child's upbringing; and
- Have given the employer the correct notice to take paternity leave.

Structure of paternity leave

Paternity leave can be taken as a single block of either one or two weeks. The definition of who qualifies for paternity leave is wide ranging and covers:

- the biological father
- someone who is married to the mother or to the 'adoptor' or
- someone who is the partner of the mother (or the adoptor) in an enduring relationship

All terms and conditions of employment remain intact during the period of paternity leave except the right to remuneration. Employees are entitled to return to the jobs they had before they took paternity leave.

Adoption leave and pay

The 2002 Employment Act creates a right for parents to take adoption leave when permanently adopting a child. An adoptive parent was entitled to take 26 weeks paid adoption leave (known as 'ordinary adoption leave') and up to 26 weeks unpaid adoption leave (this will be know as 'additional adoption leave')for children born before April 1st 2007, and 39 weeks for children born after this date. During ordinary adoption leave, employees will be entitled to receive Statutory Adoption pay (SAP) of £117.18 per week or 90% of earnings, whichever is the lower. You should check with the DTI or DSS for current rates.

Qualifying requirements

To be entitled to take adoption leave, employees must have attained 26 weeks service with their employer at the date the adoption takes place. Leave can be taken at any time after the adoption placement begins. Employees will be required to provide evidence of the adoption to the employer. Only one partner in a couple will be able to take adoption leave. The other partner, male or female, will be able to take paternity leave for 2 weeks and receive SPP. There are statutory notice provisions covering how and when employees must inform employers that they wish to take adoption leave. These are flexible and can be verified with the employer. During the period of ordinary adoption leave the employee is entitled to all their terms and conditions, except the right to remuneration. During the period of additional adoption leave, the employee is in the same position as someone on additional maternity leave – namely that whilst most of the terms and conditions of employment will be suspended, those relating to notice, confidentiality, implied terms of mutual trust and confidence, redundancy terms and disciplinary and grievance procedures will remain in place.

The right to return after either ordinary or additional adoption leave mirror's the provisions for ordinary and additional maternity leave respectively.

Health and Safety

.The law governing health and safety at work is the Health and Safety Act 1974. All employees have a statutory duty to take care of the health and safety of their employees. Foe example, they should provide first aid equipment, adequate means of escape in case of fire and protective clothing. In addition, the work place must be free of hazards. In addition, there are specific rules that govern the following:

- Cleanliness
- Noise
- Machinery
- Lifting and carrying heavy weights
- Hazardous substances
- Toilets
- Washing facilities
- Drinking water
- Seating
- First aid facilities
- Temperatures
- Hours and rests. Nearly all employees have the right not to work for more than 48 hours on average, a week. Night workers cannot work more than 8 hours per night on average in one 24-hour period. Workers aged 18 or over are entitled to one day off per week. Workers aged 16-18 are entitled to two days off per week.
- Computers

Harassment and discrimination

It is unlawful to discriminate against a person at work because of his or her:

- Sex
- Race
- Disability
- Colour
- Nationality
- Ethnic or national origin

Discrimination can either be direct or indirect. Direct discrimination occurs when a person is treated less favourably in work because of his or her sex, race or disability. Indirect discrimination occurs where a particular employee cannot meet a requirement which is not justifiable in terms of the work and is at a disadvantage, for example, if the employee only gives training to full time workers, this would indirectly discriminate against women as most part time workers are women. Another form of discrimination is harassment, which can include verbal abuse, suggestive remarks and unwanted physical contact.

Harassment/discrimination on the grounds of age, religion or sexual orientation

There is no specific law to protect someone who is being discriminated against on the grounds of age, religion or sexual orientation. However, it may be possible to argue that discrimination on the grounds of sexual orientation is sexual discrimination.

Most employers will make it policy that any such discrimination at work warrants dismissal. This will be reflected in the contract of employment.

Trade Unions

An employee has the right to join a trade union and should not be refused a job or discriminated against if this is the case. An employee also has the right not to join a trade union if they wish and should not be discriminated against on these grounds.

A member of a trade union has the right to participate in trade union activities. Any form of industrial action, i.e. going on strike is not considered a trade union activity. Trade union activities must take place either outside the individuals working hours or at a time agreed with the employer. An employee has no right in law to be paid for this work, only if it is contractually agreed.

See back of book for address of the Trade Union Congress.

Surveillance at work

Employers have a right to monitor their employee's activities in the following ways:

- Postal communications
- Telephone calls
- Faxes
- E-Mails
- Internet use
- BY CCTV use

Surveillance is only permitted by law if:

- The monitoring is relevant to the employees business
- The telecommunications system is provide for use partly or wholly in connection with the employees operation
- The employer has made all reasonable efforts to inform users that their communications will be intercepted

Ideally, an employer should have a code of conduct or policy about surveillance. If it has been agreed with the employees, it will form part of the contract of employment and can be used as a basis for disciplinary action.

If an employee believes that he or she is being monitored in a way that is not permissible then this should be challenged. To challenge surveillance at work you will probably need advice from a Citizens Advice Bureau.

8

CHILDREN AND ADULTS

The relationship between the child and the adult

At birth, the law defines a relationship between a child and his/her parent and no other adults. For many children, the law plays no further part in their upbringing. However, for others events result in the need for additional principles.

The starting point is, however, the relationship between a child and parents. Occasionally, the issue of exactly who is a parent arises.

Medical advances in assisted reproduction have caused problems which resulted in the passing of the Human Fertilisation and Embryology Act 1990, which took effect on August 1st 1991 but relates only to births after that date. There are various types of assisted reproduction, including artificial insemination, in vitro fertilisation (test tube) but as either the sperm or the embryo (or both) may be donated by strangers, it means that a child may not be genetically related to its parents.

The H.F.E.A. s 27(1) provides "where a married woman is carrying or has carried a child as a result of placing in her embryo, sperm or eggs... she is the mother of the child.

As far as the male is concerned, the rule is that the genetic father (the donor of the sperm) is the legal father. However, there are two important exceptions to this rule. First, by s 28 (2) " Where a married woman is expecting a child...notwithstanding that the sperm was not donated by the husband, he and no other person is treated as the father of the child". This section only applies if the husband consented to the wife's treatment. Second, by section 28(3) if donated sperm is used in the course of "licensed treatment" (i.e. licensed under H.F.E.A.) provided for a woman and a man together, then the man is treated as the father of the child. This section clearly covers the co-habitant of the woman.

The H.F.E.A. also deals with surrogacy, where another woman carries the child for a married couple following fertilisation. It should be noted that the Act does not apply where the surrogate is impregnated by sexual intercourse with the husband. Under s 30, the child is empowered to make an order that the child is to be treated as a child of the parties to the marriage, but the following conditions must be satisfied:

1. the parties must be married to each other and be over 18 years of age;
2. the order must be within six months of the birth;
3. the court must be satisfied that the surrogate mother and the genetic father fully understand and consent to the order;
4. the courts must also be satisfied that no money changed hands in connection with the arrangements but reasonable expenses are allowed (clothes, travel etc).

Paternity disputes
Unless paternity is admitted it must be proved. Such an issue could arise within a number of different types of proceedings and the courts will often need to determine the paternity of the child as a preliminary matter.

The question of paternity can also be dealt with as an issue in its own right. Under the Family Law Act 1996, a person can apply to the court simply for a declaration that a named person is the father.

Paternity can be established in a number of different ways, for example, evidence may be adduced of out of court admission by the man; of the fact that the man is registered as the father in the Register of Births Deaths and Marriages; of the man having had sexual intercourse with the mother at the time that conception must have taken place.

Conclusions drawn from the results of blood tests have also been given as evidence. The advent of DNA fingerprinting has strengthened this method. This can be used on any type of human tissue and can provide virtually conclusive proof of paternity. It is only of use if all parties, mother, child and alleged father are tested. The Family Law Reform Act 1969 provides that, where parentage is an issue, the court may order that a person or party to the proceedings submit to a blood test.

Status of children
The legal effect of the physical relationship between parent and child is

sometimes dependent upon whether the child was born to married or unmarried parents. At common law, a child born to unmarried parents had no rights against his father and remoter ancestors and, to begin with, no rights even against his mother Changes in the law have eroded that position. Amendments in the legal position of the child born to unmarried parents have been affected by either extending the categories of children who were to be taken as having been born to married parents or by specifically providing that those born to unmarried parents should have some of the same rights as those born to married parents.

Nevertheless, prior to the FLRA there still existed some significant differences in the legal positions of the two categories of children. The Act was designed to eradicate those differences as much as was thought reasonable. It was also designed to discourage the practice of labeling children as legitimate or illegitimate, which is accepted as outmoded terminology.

Parental responsibility

However, with the exception of adoption before the advent of the Children's Act 1989, the law was very complex indeed, and, with any order relating to the upbringing of children, all orders have been replaced by the provisions of the Children's Act. The Children's Act, drawing on cases before its inception, would define parental responsibility as follows:

a) to have possession of the child and to take, on its behalf, all the many and minor decisions that arise every day;
b) to maintain contact with the child;
c) to actively consider and provide for the child's education;
d) to actively consider the need and provide for medical treatment on the child's behalf;
e) to administer the child's property;
f) to actively consider the wisdom of and consent or otherwise to the child's marriage between the age of 16-18;
g) to protect the child from physical and moral danger;
h) to maintain the child financially.

To whom does parental responsibility belong?

At the birth of a child, the position is as follows: the parental responsibility of a child born to married parents belongs to both parents (section 2(1)); the parental responsibility for children born to unmarried parents belongs exclusively to the mother (section 2(2)).

Section 4, however, provides two methods whereby parental responsibility between unmarried parents shall be made; they are the agreement to share parental responsibility (between parents) which must be in writing, in the prescribed form and recorded with the principal Registry of the Family Division. The alternative is that the father may apply to the court, who can order that he shall share the parental responsibility of the child with the mother.

Parental responsibility, or a large part of it, can be obtained by persons other than the parents of a child. For example, a parent, with parental responsibility may, in writing, appoint a guardian for his child and such an appointment vests parental responsibility in the guardian. Further, there are a number of court orders which have the effect of vesting parental responsibility in the person awarded the order, e.g. a residence order.

The termination of parental responsibility

Apart from the appointment of a guardian or an agreement between married parents, it is impossible for a person with parental responsibility to voluntarily surrender the whole or any part of it to another. The exercise of it may be delegated to a third party however.

Parental responsibility is not lost as a result of some other person acquiring it.

Subject to what is said below, parental responsibility can only be terminated by court order and only where this is specifically provided for.

For parents married when their child was born, and an unmarried mother, parental responsibility can only be terminated by the grant of an adoption order in favour of someone else. Adoption also has this effect on others who have acquired parental responsibility. Further, their parental responsibility can be terminated by an order revoking or discharging the instrument, agreement or order that gave them parental responsibility.

Parental responsibility is owed to a child, defined by the Children's Act, as a person under 18 (save for certain aspects of financial responsibility). Thus, generally, parental responsibility terminates automatically when the child reaches 18.

Children of the family
By section 105, the term a child of the family, 'in relation to parties to a marriage means:

a) a child of both parties;
b) any other child, being a child who is placed with the parties as foster parents....who has been treated by both of the parties as a child of the family'.

It can be seen that this is a relationship between a child and adults who are married to each other. The adults could be the child's natural parents but need not be. One of the adults could be a natural parent and the other not, or both adults could have no blood tie with the child at all.

The relationship is significant in that financial awards can be made in favour of such a child against the adults. The relationship does not result in the adults having parental responsibility for the child: if the adults, or one of them, are the child's parents, they or he will have parental responsibility due to parenthood, not as a result of the child being a child of the family. But the existence of this relationship does give adults who are not the child's parents some preferential treatment, they being entitled to apply for some of the Children Act Orders discussed in this book.

Principles used by the courts to determine orders
By section 1 (5) the court is enjoined not to make an order under the C.A. unless it considers that doing so would better for the child than making no order at all. This principle was new to the C.A. and was in line with the Law Commission recommendations. It was felt that it was better for the child if the parents could agree on the arrangements for him or her. There was also the view that the courts intervention exacerbated rather than improved the situation, though it is still not clear if the non intervention principle has made any difference in that regard.

The Welfare Principle

When determining any question relating to a child's upbringing or the administration of his property or income, the most fundamental principle is that the child's welfare is the court's paramount consideration.

The Welfare Checklist

For specific guidance on welfare, the court must take into account a statutory list of guidelines contained in section 1 (3), they being as follows:

a)   the ascertainable wishes and feelings of the child (considered in the light of his age and understanding);

b) his physical, emotional and educational needs

c)   the likely effect on him of any change in his circumstances-stability in the life of a child is considered beneficial;

d) his age, sex and background and any other characteristics that the court considers relevant;

e) any harm he has suffered or is at risk of suffering, both physical and emotional;

f)   how capable each of his parents are, and any other person in relation to whom the court considers the question to be relevant, of meeting the child's needs;

g)   the range of powers available to the courts under the C.A. in the proceedings in question.

All of the above factors must be taken into account when considering the application for the grant of an order.

Children's rights

Although it is recognised that a child clearly has rights, the overriding principle of the Children's Act is to ensure that the welfare of the child is catered for.

This means, in practice, often over ruling the child's wishes and feelings and that decisions are quite often taken without reference to the child at all.

Resolution of disputes between private individuals

A new guardianship scheme has been created by the Children's Act ss 5 and 6 and a new parental responsibility order for unmarried fathers. There are four new orders created by s 8 of the Children's Act, Section 8 Orders:

1.Residence Order;

2.Contact Order;

3.A Prohibited Steps Order;

4.A Specific Issues Order.

Residence order

This is an order that settles the arrangements to be made as to the person with whom the child is to live. It can be made in favour of any person, with the exception of the local authority. It can be made in favour of more than one person specifying periods of time spent with individuals if they do not live together.

In many cases, the person with parental responsibility will be granted the order. However, it is the person to whom the order is granted who assumes responsibility.

Contact Order

This is an order requiring the person with whom the child resides to allow the child to visit or stay with another [person. Again, local authorities are excluded.

Prohibited Steps Order

This is an order directing a person named in the order not to take any specified step in relation to the child without the permission of the court.

Specific Issues Order

This is an order that determines a specific question in connection with any aspect of parental responsibility. An example may mean schools attended, religion etc. Section 8 orders can be made subject to directions as to their implementation and conditions that must be complied with. None of these orders can be made once a child has reached his 16th birthday or extend beyond then unless there are exceptional circumstances (s9(6) and (7).

Different types of proceedings

The only way for private individuals to take steps to resolve disputes concerning bringing up a child is for one of them to issue proceeding under the Children's Act. Like the above orders, the Children's Act has greatly simplified dispute resolution. The only exceptions to this relate to wardship and adoption.

Under the Children's Act it is possible to apply for an order appointing a guardian of the child (s 5). An order of this type gives parental responsibility. It is also possible for an unmarried father to apply far an order that gives him parental responsibility. The main type of application possible under the Children Act however, is a section 8 order.

An application for such an order can be made in several ways, either as a "free standing application" or as part of "family proceedings" Section 8 defines "family proceedings" The list includes jurisdictions which used to have their own powers to grant orders relating to upbringing of children, for example the M.C.A. It also includes applications under part one of the Children's Act itself. It should be noted that once family proceedings have commenced, the court can make a section 8 order itself, of its own motion.

Types of applicant

In most cases, it is the parents of the child who are in dispute about its upbringing. However, others with an interest in the child's welfare may also make an application. The Children Act recognises the need for persons other than parents of a child to be able to get orders that relate to the child's upbringing. Those entitled to apply for any s 8 order:

1. A parent or guardian of the child;
2. A person who has been granted a residence order.

Those entitled to apply for a residence or contact order:
1. A spouse or ex spouse in relation to whom the child is a child of the family;

2. A person with whom the child has lived for at least three years. This need not be continuous as long as the period does not begin more than five years, nor end more than three months before, the making of the application;

3. A person who has the consent of the person in whose favour there is a residence order, if one has been granted, the local authority if the child is in care and in any other case any other person with parental responsibility.

The factors a court must take into account when considering making an order are designed to prevent applications deemed not to be serious and also possibly injurious to the child's future well-being. They include the nature of the persons connection with a child (s 10 (9).

Protection of children
Types of orders available
Before the Children's Act came into being, there were many types of orders available to local authorities which enabled them to offer some form of protection to children. Local authorities could, on passing a specific resolution, assume the role of parent.

The Children's Act makes an attempt to get rid of the uncertainty of the old laws. It replaced all the old laws and replaced them with a new scheme. In addition, local authorities can no longer pass a parental rights resolution. No child may be taken into care without a court order.

The following orders are available:

1.Care orders (s 31);

2. Supervision orders (s 31);

3.The education supervision order (s 36);

4.The emergency protection order (s 44);

5.The child assessment order (s 43).

Care orders
This is an order that commits a child into the care of a local authority. It cannot be made in favour of anyone else. The effect of a care order is that the child in question goes to live in a local authority community home, or with local authority foster parents. The legal effect is that the local authority gains parental responsibility for the child while the order is in force. A care order automatically brings to an end any residence order that exists. But if a parent or guardian has parental responsibility at the time that a care order comes into force, this continues. A care order cannot be made in respect of a child who has reached 17 (16 if married). It lasts until the age of 18.

Supervision orders
This is an order placing the child under the supervision of a local authority or probation officer. This order does not carry any parental responsibility and there is no power to take a child from his home. A supervision order can have conditions attached to it as the court sees fit. A supervision order cannot be made in respect of a child who has reached the age of 17 (16 if married). Generally, a supervision order has a life span of one year but can be extended to two years.

Education supervision orders
This is an order placing a child under the supervision of the local education authority.

Emergency protection orders
These orders usually take time to activate. For those children requiring emergency protection the above order is issued. It is an order that empowers the local authority or NSPCC to remove a child from its home and also gives the local authority parental responsibility.

Applications can be made ex-parte, without the necessity of informing or involving the child's parents or any other person. In this way, it is possible to obtain the court order very quickly indeed.

The order lasts for eight days only and can be extended for a further seven days. After 72 hours, an application for its discharge can be made.

The child assessment order

This order is a new concept, the above replacing orders already in existence. Although a local authority may feel that a child is at risk there are times when it cannot gain access to the child to compile evidence. In the past the local authority could apply for a place of safety order and remove the child immediately from its home. It could also do nothing.

The child assessment order has effect for seven days maximum. With such an order it is possible to remove a child from its home. There is no parental responsibility. The intention behind the order is to enable the local authority to assess the child so it can make the necessary arrangements after consideration.

Before the Children's Act came into being, it was possible to make orders giving a local authority the right to intervene in a child's life under a number of jurisdictions, some overlapping. The Children's Act is now the only jurisdiction under which a local authority may act. By section 31 (4) an application for a care order or a supervision order can be made on its own or within family proceedings as defined by section 8 (3) of the Act. Applications for education supervision orders, emergency protection orders and child assessment orders have to made alone.

Categories of applicants for orders are limited to the following:
Care orders, supervision orders and child assessment orders-only a local authority or NSPCC may apply.

Education supervision orders-only a local education authority may apply.

Emergency protection orders-only a local authority may apply.

In place of previous powers to make different orders, the court now has intermediate powers under section 37. Where a court is dealing with family proceedings in which a question relating to the welfare of a child arises, it may direct the local authority to carry out investigations. The local authority must respond and decide what order should be applied for. If the local authority decides not to apply for an order the court cannot make it do so, although this fact must be reported to the court.

Grounds on which a court will grant an order

A court has to be satisfied of the following before granting an order:
(a) that the child has suffered or is likely to suffer significant harm;
(b) that the harm or likelihood of harm is attributable to the care given to the child, or likely to be given to him if the order were not made or the child being beyond parental control.

Proof of the ground in section 31(2) only entitles a court to grant a care or supervision order. The court does not have to grant such an order. The grounds in this section are referred to as "threshold" grounds.

In relation to education and supervision orders, the court has to be satisfied that the child is of compulsory school age and not being properly educated.

To obtain an emergency protection order, the local authority must demonstrate the following:

(a) a local authority must show that the enquiries are being frustrated and that access to the child is required urgently;
(b) the NSPCC must show that it has reasonable cause to suspect that the child is in danger of suffering significant harm;
(c) any other applicant must show that there is reasonable cause to believe that the child is likely to suffer significant harm if he is not removed from the home.

As with the other orders, applications for emergency protection orders are subject to section 1 of the Act. For child assessment orders, the court has to be satisfied that:

a) the applicant has reasonable cause to suspect that the child is suffering or likely to suffer significant harm;

(b) this can only be determined by an assessment of the child's health or development;

(c) it is not likely that an assessment can be made without an order.

Again, applications for this order are subject to section 1 of the children Act.

Parental contact

By section 34 of the Act a local authority is under a duty to allow reasonable contact between a child in care and his parents. If there is any dispute on the reasonableness of contact, the court can regulate. In limited circumstances, a local authority can refuse to allow contact for up to seven days.

By section 43, if a child is to be kept away from home during the currency of the child assent order, the order must contain directions for such contact between the child and other persons as the court thinks fit.

By section 44, an applicant who is granted such an order is placed under a duty to allow reasonable contact between child and parents.

Wardship

Wardship is the means by which the family court fulfils its jurisdiction of protection of children. When a child becomes a ward of court, the court controls its upbringing by a series of orders.

9

PROVIDING FINANCIALLY FOR CHILDREN

In July 1990, the Government announced the setting up of the Child Support Agency, brought into being by the Child Support Act 1991. The purpose of the agency was to improve on the then existing child maintenance system that, according to the government allowed errant fathers to avoid maintenance with no real sanctions. The Government stated:

"The present system is unnecessarily fragmented, uncertain in its results, slow and in effective. It is largely based on discretion. The cumulative effect is uncertainty and inconsistent decisions about how much maintenance should be paid".

The C.S.A came into force on April 5th 1993. The agency is responsible for all new cases, cases where the claimant is on income support and family credit. In 1995, in response to further criticism, the government introduced further legislation in the Child Support Act 1995.

The principle of the C.S.A. is that whatever the changes in parents relationships, they cannot change their responsibility towards their children. There is a formula laid out which fixes maintenance levels and Child Support Officers have wide powers to collect information.

The C.S.A applies to a "qualifying Child" defined by section 3(1) of the Act as a child where one or both of his parents is an "absent" parent. This means a parent who is not living in the same household as the child, notwithstanding contact arrangements. The person with whom the child has a home is called 'a person with care'. The Act only applies to children aged sixteen or under or nineteen or under and in full time education..

The C.S.A applies only to natural or adoptive parents or persons treated as parents under the H.F.E.A (Human Fertilisation and Embryology Act 1990). The absent parent is required to make periodical payments in accordance with fixed criteria.

The C.S.A. lays down a maintenance requirement, the amount needed to maintain the child based on income support criteria. There is a maintenance assessment that is the assessable income of the absent parent, adding the income of person with care and dividing by two.

There is also an additional element whereby the absent parent can be called upon to contribute further up to a statutory maximum. There is also a protected income level that is designed to ensure that the absent parent is better off than he would be on income support.

Once the assessment is made, the Agency may carry out collections and enforcement and will automatically do so where the claimant is on income support.

The Agency may make deductions from earnings orders under S31, and may apply to the Magistrates for a liability order under S33, and in the event of willful refusal or culpable neglect, imprisonment for up to six weeks under section 40.

S9(1) states that no agreement for maintenance can prevent a person with care from applying for an assessment and any clause purporting to exclude that right is void.

The maintenance assessment can only be made on application to the agency, but in respect of persons with care on benefit, they must authorise action on penalty of a reduction in benefit under section 46(5) of 20% for 26 weeks followed by 10% for a further year. Under s6(2) the requirement to co-operate may be waived if an officer is satisfied that there is a risk to a claimant or any child of, suffering harm or distress. Maintenance assessments and special cases Regulations 1992 give relief to an absent parent who has regular contact with his child.

The assessment is reduced if the child spends 104 nights or more each year with the absent parents. Since April 1995, recognition has been given to take account of the need of the absent parent who had transferred capital, usually in the form of the matrimonial home, to the parent with care. This has been achieved by giving the absent parent a further allowance calculated rateably according to the value of the property transferred. The 1995 Act seeks to incorporate greater flexibility into the scheme, by means of a series of departure directions which the secretary of state may influence if two conditions are fulfilled:

a) the case falls within one or more of the cases set out in part 1 of schedule 4; and

b) it is his opinion that it would be just and equitable to give the departure direction.

The overall effect will be to permit the agency to take account of certain circumstances, such as additional expenses borne by the absent parent, the fact that the absent parent has transferred property to the parent with care or that the parent with care is not utilising an asset to maximise its income producing potential so as to reduce the maintenance assessment which would otherwise be payable. The additional expenses include:

- costs incurred in long distance travelling to work;
- costs incurred by an absent parent in maintaining contact with the child;
- debts incurred before the parent became an absent parent in relation to the child. Though 'debts' are not defined, certain debts are excluded, including gambling debts, trade or business debts or use of credit cards;
- pre-1993 commitments which it is impossible, or it would be unreasonable to expect the parent concerned to withdraw from;
- costs incurred by a parent in supporting a child who is not his, but is part of his family.

Each are subject to rigorous conditions before it can qualify for consideration.

Few would argue with the CSA that parents are financially responsible for their children but the lack of flexibility in the calculation, the absence of appeals and the disregard for previous arrangements have caused exceptional hardship for some parents who have second families or who have made clean break settlements prior to the introduction of the CSA.

Although the C.S.A. supplants the courts powers, the sections of the Matrimonial Causes Act 1973 and Children's Act 1989 are not repealed and the provisions are still relevant. Courts have a role in the following circumstances:

a) Where the absent parent is sufficiently wealthy to be able to top up the maximum maintenance under the CSA.

b) Where the child is receiving full time instruction or training requiring provision of some or all of the expenses, e.g. school fees.

c) Where the child is disabled, orders may be made to meet some or all of the expenses attributable to that disability.

d) Where 17 and 18 year olds are not in full time education.

e) Where there is a lump sum or transfer of property order.

f) Where the child is a "child of the family" and not a qualifying child.

Matrimonial Causes Act 1973
Within the framework of the above children can have the same types of orders made in their favour, against either of the parties to the marriage as can the parties themselves. The order can direct payment to the child or third party. generally, no application for an order in favour of a child over 18 can be made.

Periodical payments orders secured or unsecured must terminate when the child reaches 17 unless the court decides to the contrary. Both types of payments must cease on the death of the payer.

Matters taken into account when making an order
As with spouse orders, the first consideration of the court, when deciding whether and how to exercise it powers, is the welfare of any minor children of the family.

The courts, under M.C.A. s 25(3) will have regard to:

a) the financial needs of the child

b) the income, earning capacity, property and other financial resources of the child

c) any physical or mental disability of the child

d) the type of education or training he was receiving or was expected to receive by the parties to the marriage

e) the financial assets and needs of the parties, the standard of living enjoyed by the family prior to the breakdown of the marriage and any physical or mental disability of the parties.

The M.C.A. s 25(4) provides further factors to be taken into account when the court is considering making an order against a party to the marriage who is not a parent of the child, and include, for example the liability of any other person to maintain the child.

The Children Act 1989, Section 15

Section 15 of the CA provides for the grant of a range of financial and property awards for children subject to the C.S.A. The applicant must be the parent or guardian of the child and orders can be made against the parent. It must be remembered that the availability of these orders is not dependent upon the parties being married to each other, it is dependent upon parenthood. However, married parents may make use of section 15 where there is no pending divorce proceedings.

The court has the power to make the following orders:

a) that either parent pay periodical payments for the benefit of the child, secured or unsecured
b) that either parent pay a lump sum for the benefit of the child
c) that either parent transfer property to which he is entitled to the child

d) that either parent do settle such property for the benefit of the child.

Payments and transfer for the benefit of the child can be ordered to be made direct to the child or to some third party. It should be noted that if applications
are made to magistrates courts, the only orders that can be made are ones for unsecured periodical payments and lump sums not exceeding £1,000.

All the above orders benefit children alone. Orders for unsecured periodical payments cease on the death of the payer and for both types of periodical payments the rules for cessation when the child reaches a specific age apply.

The CA schedule one lists the matters that the court must take into account when deciding what order to make. They bear some similarity to those listed in the M.C.A. s 25(3), the factors relevant for child orders ancillary to decree proceedings.

10

THE LAW OF DIVORCE

Divorce law has developed over the years through legislation made by Parliament and through the build up of "precedents" or through cases decided by the courts. However, in the last thirty years there have been fundamental changes in the way society, and the law, has come to view divorce.

Modern divorce law recognizes that "Irretrievable breakdown" of a marriage should be the one and only ground for divorce. This recognition signalled a move away from the idea of "guilty parties" in divorce.

Before the introduction of the notion of irretrievable breakdown it was held that one party had to prove that the other party was guilty of destroying the marriage before divorce could be granted. The law is now much more flexible in its recognition of the breakdown of a marriage.

Since the present law was introduced, making it much easier to obtain divorce, the number of marriage breakdowns in Britain has risen significantly, with one in three couples in Britain filing for divorce. This is currently the highest rate in Europe.

There are a lot of problems associated with the law, and the role of those who make divorce law generally. The whole question of divorce law is under scrutiny, particularly the question of whether or not the law should attempt to keep marriages intact or whether it should seek to ease the transition to final separation without presenting unnecessary obstacles.

However, although we hear periodic announcements from different politicians on the importance of keeping the family unit intact, and by implication making it harder for people to divorce, the whole climate has changed over the years whereby the law seems to be the facilitator of divorce as opposed to dictating whether or not people can get a divorce.

There has also been a major shift in the law concerning children of divorcing couples. Under The Children Act of 1989 (as amended), parents in divorce proceedings are encouraged to take the initiative and take matters into their own hands, making their own decisions concerning the child's future life after divorce. The courts role has been greatly restricted.

The Child Support Act 1991 (as amended by the 1995 CSA) has also dramatically changed the role of the courts in divorce proceedings. After April 1993, maintenance applications are no longer a matter for the courts but for a new government agency, the Child Support Agency, which assesses and determines applications for maintenance in accordance with a set formula. The courts will only now deal with applications for maintenance in certain circumstances.

The courts

Before looking at the law surrounding divorce in greater depth we should look briefly at the structure of the courts and how divorce law is administered. Most divorces are handled by a branch of the County Court system known as the Divorce County Courts. Not all county courts are able to deal with divorce, those that can are known as divorce county courts. Decisions concerning divorce cases, and subsequent orders, are made by Judges and District Judges. These people are appointed from the ranks of senior lawyers.

In London, the equivalent of the divorce county court is known as the "Divorce Registry" and is based in the Royal Courts of Justice in the Strand.

The High Court

Sometimes, rarely, divorce cases need to be referred to the High Court. There are several sections of the high court-the section responsible for divorce and other similar matters is known as the Family Division. However, the majority of divorce cases will be heard in the County Courts.

Hearing your divorce case

Hearings related to divorce cases are either in "Open" court or in "Chambers". Proceedings in open court are heard in the courtroom itself. They are usually formal and members of the public are allowed to attend.

However, most divorces are heard in chambers. These proceedings are private and the general public has no right to attend or listen. Only those people directly concerned with the case are allowed to attend.

Seeking a divorce – the grounds for divorce

The first question facing couples wishing to divorce is whether or not they qualify at the outset to bring proceedings, i.e., what are the ground rules.

If one or other parties wishes to file for divorce, the most basic requirement that must be fulfilled is that they should have been married for one-year minimum. They must also be "domiciled" in this country, i.e., England is regarded as their home. Alternatively, they must have been resident in England for one year before the date on which proceedings are brought.

A court can halt proceedings for divorce in England if it would be better for the case to be heard in another country. Usually, the court would try to decide which country is the most appropriate, or with which country the divorcing couple are most closely associated.

Grounds for divorce – the five facts.

As we have seen, there is only one ground for granting a divorce, that is the irretrievable breakdown of marriage. Fundamentally, this means that your marriage has broken down to such a degree that it cannot be retrieved and the only solution is to end it legally.

The person, or spouse, who requests a divorce is known as the "petitioner". the other party is known as the "respondent". Although there is only one ground for divorce, the court has to be satisfied that there is clear evidence of one of the following five facts:

1. that the respondent has committed adultery and the petitioner cannot, or finds it intolerable, to live with the respondent;

2. that the respondent has behaved in such a way that you cannot reasonably be expected to live with him or her (unreasonable behaviour)

3. that the respondent has deserted you for a continuous period of two years immediately before the presentation of your petition for divorce.

4. that parties to a marriage have lived apart for more than two years prior to filing for divorce and that there is no objection or defence to filing for divorce. This is known as the "no fault" ground;

5. that parties to marriage have lived apart continuously five years prior to filing for divorce.

Since the advent of the 1996 Family Law Act, it has been proposed that the above five facts are replaced with a single ground for divorce. However, although the Act came into force in July 1997, the changes to the divorce procedures have yet to be effected. Therefore, from hereon, we will refer to the practice as it currently stands.

We should now look at each of these "five facts" in more depth.

1. Adultery

Quite simply, adultery is defined as heterosexual sex between one party to a marriage and someone else. Oddly enough, because the law states quite clearly heterosexual sex, then gay or lesbian sex cannot (in theory) constitute adultery. Adultery usually means that a "full" sexual act has been committed so therefore if there has not been penetration then this will not be seen to be adulterous.

For adultery to be proved, an admission by the respondent or evidence of adultery is usually sufficient. The co-respondent need not be named in the divorce petition. If you do mention the name of the co-respondent involved in the adultery, that person is entitled to take part in the divorce proceedings in so far as they affect them. The court will provide the co-respondent with copies of all the relevant divorce papers and he or she will have the opportunity to confirm or deny anything said about him or her in the divorce proceedings.

Proving adultery is the first step. You then have to satisfy the courts that you find it intolerable to live with the respondent any further. However, it is not essential to prove that you find it intolerable to live with

94

the respondent because of their adultery. It may be that your marriage has been unhappy for some time and that the adulterous act has proven to be the end.

If, after you discover the respondent's adultery, you continue to live together as man and wife for a period of six months or more, you will not be able to rely on adultery as a reason for divorce. As long as the periods of living together after the adultery do not exceed six months in total, the courts will completely disregard them. This gives some room for attempts at reconciliation.

Unreasonable behaviour

Although "unreasonable behaviour" is a commonly cited fact for divorce, in practice the court has stringent criteria, which must be met before this is accepted. The law actually says that you must demonstrate that your spouse has behaved in such a way that you cannot reasonably be expected to continue to live with that person.

The court considering your case will look at the particular circumstances surrounding your situation and will then decide whether or not you should continue to tolerate your partner's behaviour within marriage.

The main principle underlying unreasonable behaviour is that it is particular to your own situation and that it cannot be seen as relative to other people's behaviour. You must prove that the behaviour of your partner has gone well beyond the kind of day-to-day irritations that many people suffer and there is real reason to grant a divorce.

Examples of such behaviour range from continuous violence and threatening or intimidating behaviour, drunkenness, sexual perversions, neglect, and imposing unreasonable restrictions on another person.

Desertion

The fact that you must prove that your spouse has deserted you for a continuous period of two years can present difficulties.

If you are seeking a divorce on the basis of desertion, then it is likely that you will need to employ a solicitor who will need to check rigorously that you comply with the often-complex requirements upon which a court will insist before granting a divorce. In the main, desertion has arisen because of other associated problems within marriage, and therefore this factor can often be joined with others when applying for a divorce

The simplest form of desertion is when one person walks out on another for no apparent reason. Desertion, however, is not just a physical separation of husband and wife. It implies that the deserting party has rejected all the normal obligations associated with marriage.

Before desertion is proven a court will need to be satisfied of two things:

1. you must demonstrate that you and your spouse have been living separately for a continuous period of two years immediately before you started the divorce proceedings. Although it is usual for separation to start when one person leaves the marital home, it can also happen whilst you are living under the same roof, but living totally separate lives.

The courts are very rigorous indeed when determining that this is the case and will need to be satisfied that your lives are indeed separate and that you can no longer go on carrying out functions jointly.

The court will disregard short periods during the separation where you may have attempted to patch up your differences. However, for example, if you attempt to reconcile six months into the initial two year period and this lasts for two months before you separate again, although the courts will not make you start again they will make you wait a further two months before they will hear your divorce. Therefore, the two years becomes two years and two months.

2. that your spouse has decided that your marriage is over-you must also be able to demonstrate that when he or she stopped living with you, your spouse viewed the marriage as ended and intended to separate from you on a permanent basis.

You will not be able to claim desertion if you consented to the separation. The court will take consent to mean that you made it clear from the outset that you consented to separation, through your words or actions. In addition, you will not be able to claim desertion if your spouse had perfectly good reason to leave, for example he or she may have gone abroad with your full knowledge, to work or may have entered hospital for a long period. If your spouse leaves because of your own unreasonable behaviour, then you cannot claim desertion. If you are to blame in this case, the courts will not accept desertion.

Finally, because the courts see desertion as essentially separation against your will, then if you come back together again on a permanent basis you can no longer claim desertion.

Separation for two years with consent

As with desertion, the particular circumstances in which the law looks upon you as having been separated for two years can include periods of time where you may have been under the same roof together but not functioning as a married couple. There may be short periods during this time where you have lived together, for example, an attempt at reconciliation.

However, as with desertion you will not be able to count these periods towards the two years separation. Therefore, if you have a trial reconciliation period for three months then you will have to wait two years and three months before you can apply for divorce.

The fundamental difference between desertion and separation with consent is that you would not be granted a divorce on the basis of separation if your spouse did not give his or her consent to the divorce.

The court has rigid criteria for proving that your spouse consents to the divorce. Consent is only seen as valid if your spouse has freely given it without pressure. There must also be full understanding on his or her part of what a divorce will mean and how it will affect his or her life.

The court sends a form to divorcing parties soon after initial divorce papers are filed, together with explanatory notes and it is at this point when your spouse will give consent.

If your spouse will not consent to divorce and you cannot prove either desertion or adultery then you will be in the position where you will have to wait until five years separation has elapsed before you can seek a divorce.

In relation to the above, i.e., divorces granted on the basis of two years separation and consent or five years separation, the courts can exercise special powers to ensure that the financial and personal position of the respondent is protected. The courts can sometimes delay the process of divorce, or even prevent it, to make sure that there is no undue suffering or exploitation.

Five years separation

The final of the "five facts" is the fact of five years separation. If you have been separated for five or more years the courts will grant a divorce whether or not the other party agrees to it, subject to what has been said above.

Again, the courts will allow for a period of attempted reconciliation up to six months and the same rules concerning length of time apply as with the other facts. Should you live together for longer than six months, the courts will demand that you start the five-year period again.

Reconciliation

As been shown, in all the provisions of the law relating to each of the five facts, which have to be demonstrated in addition to the main ground of "irretrievable breakdown", there are built in provisions for reconciliation. The law is fairly flexible when taking into account attempts at reconciling and sorting out differences.

In effect, these built in provisions allow for a period of up to six months in which both parties can make a concerted attempt at solving their problems. If these attempts are unsuccessful then their legal position vis-a-vis divorce proceedings will not be jeopardized. The reconciliation provisions apply for a period up to six months or separate periods not exceeding six months.

In addition to this, a solicitor, if you have one, will need to certify that he or she has discussed the possibility of reconciliation with you and has ensured that both parties know where to seek advice and guidance if they really wish to attempt reconciliation.

The court, if it so wishes, can also adjourn proceedings to give both parties further time to decide whether they genuinely wish to make a further effort to prolong their marriage.

At the end of this book can be found names and addresses of various organizations, which can help with the process of reconciliation. The best known of these is RELATE.

Conciliation and mediation services

There is a fundamental difference between reconciliation, and those services, which offer help, and conciliation and mediation services. Conciliation is directed towards making parting easier to handle. The role of the conciliator is to sort out at least some of the difficulties between those who have made a definite and firm decision to obtain a divorce.

The process of conciliation can take place either out of court, or in court. In court conciliation only arises once the process of litigating for divorce has commenced. It is particularly relevant where the future of children is under discussion. With in-court conciliation, there is usually what is known as a "pre trial review of the issues and problems which parties to a divorce are unable to settle them. Both the court welfare officer and the district judge are involved in this process. Out of court conciliation and mediation is intended to assist both parties in reaching an agreement at a stage before they arrive in court, or approach the court. The person involved at this stage is usually always professionally trained, a social worker normally, and who will act as go between.

Both parties can also use specially trained legal personnel, lawyers to help them reach an agreement. This process is like the process of arbitration and is intended to make the formal legal proceedings less hostile and acrimonious.

Since the advent of the Family Law Act 1996, much more emphasis has been put on mediation and reconciliation, indeed this will be a central plank of the proposed new divorce process, when it finally comes into being.

Commencing proceedings
Using a solicitor
Although it makes sense to take legal advice when taking your first steps towards divorce, there is no rule that says you have to.

It is important to examine the role of the solicitor, in the first instance, in order to get an idea of the advantages.

The amount of advice you will need from a solicitor will depend entirely on the circumstances of your case and the complexities involved.

Most divorces will have two fairly distinct stages - the first step of obtaining the divorce decree (divorce) and the more complicated problems of sorting out property and financial matters and making arrangements concerning children.

As with most county court procedures now, the procedure for commencing divorce and the subsequent steps up to the issuing of a decree is largely paperwork. Provided that the circumstances of your divorce are straightforward then there is no real need to consult a solicitor at all.

It is up to both parties to ascertain the complexity of the divorce before deciding to go it alone. The questions you should be asking yourselves, preferably during a face-to-face meeting, are whether or not the marriage can be ended with the minimum of problems.

If you are childless and there is no property at stake and there will be no financial complications then you should be able to proceed without a solicitor.

If, however, you own property and have children and also have life insurance policies and pension schemes etc, then you will need to try to reach agreement concerning the division of these. This is where divorce gets complicated and may entail you requesting legal advice.

The division of your assets is a matter for you but it has to be reached by agreement.

One other aspect of do-it-yourself divorce is that it can be time consuming. Some people cannot spare the valuable time involved and will be happier to leave it to a solicitor.

A solicitor will handle the whole matter for you, when instructed, from obtaining initial information you to obtaining a decree. Your main input will be to check over the necessary paperwork at each stage, as required and, in certain cases to deliver documents to the court. However, all of this will be done at the request and direction of the solicitor.

Your future arrangements

Whilst not essential to consult a solicitor, it is wise to at least get a view on future arrangements which you have negotiated. This is particularly important when it comes to future tax arrangements.

If it is necessary to ask a court to determine future arrangements, because of the inability of parties to a divorce to agree or negotiate, then a solicitor will need to take charge of the whole process. Remember, the more a solicitor does for you the more it will cost. You should both bear this in mind when beginning discussions.

An outline of divorce procedure

In undefended petitions, both spouses accept that the divorce will go ahead. In defended petitions, one party is filing a defence against the petition.

A special procedure was introduced to deal with undefended divorce petitions, primarily because of the large volume of cases presented to the courts.

At present, there is a set pattern, which you must follow if you wish to obtain a divorce:

a) the petition must be filled in

b) the petition must enclose a statement of arrangements for the children.

c) the petition must be sent to the registrar of the divorce county court.

d) there must be sufficient copies for the other parties to the divorce.

e) the respondent will then receive his or her copies from the court.

f) other parties involved will receive their copies.

g) the respondent must, on a prescribed form, acknowledge service.

h) the respondent must make clear that he or she has no intention to defend.

i) the documents are examined by a court official (the divorce registrar)

j) the divorce registrar then certifies that the facts of the case are approved.
k) the judge pronounces the decree nisi in open court.

l) the decree is made absolute on application by the petitioner.
Each of the above steps will be discussed briefly below.

The preparation of the divorce petition.
Either you or your solicitor will prepare the divorce petition. This document can be obtained from HMSO or a sample can be obtained from the county court and will form the basis of your claim for a divorce.

On this form you will record details of your marriage and your children and the grounds on which you are seeking a divorce. You will also list the claims that you are asking the court to consider. This part is particularly important. For example you may wish the court to consider financial matters for you.

Normally, you would include your address on the form but you can make application to the court to leave out your address if this poses any danger to you.

It is of the utmost importance that you take care at this stage because you are asking the court to make a very important decision on the basis of information given. You should avoid exaggerating the truth.

The statement of arrangements
If there are children involved you must fill in another document known simply as "statement of arrangements for children" This sets out the arrangements you intend to make for children once the divorce is granted.

A child, for the purposes of the court is any child who is a child of both parties, an adopted child, or any other child who has been treated by both as part of your family. This does not include children boarded out by local authorities or social services or other voluntary organizations.

Although the courts are not generally concerned with the welfare of adult children (over 16) you will be required to give details of children under 18 who are still receiving instruction at an educational establishment or undergoing other training such as for trade or profession.

The information required for the statement of arrangements will be:

a) where the children will live after divorce
b) who else will be residing there
c) who will look after them
d) where they are to be educated
e) what financial arrangements have been proposed for them
f) what arrangements have been made for the other parent to see them
g) whether they have any illness or disability
i) whether they are under the care or supervision of a person or organization (i.e. social services)

When you have completed this form your spouse should be in agreement. If she or he is not then there will be an opportunity at a later stage to make alternative proposals to the court.

Filing the papers with the court
The court office requires the following to commence proceedings:
a) the completed divorce petition (copy for spouse)
b) Completed statement of arrangements if appropriate, plus copy for spouse
c) a copy of your marriage certificate
d) In certain cases a fee if you are not receiving help under the legal help scheme
e) Once received in court the case will be given a reference number.

Serving the papers
Once the petition has been received by the courts the court office will then send a copy plus copy of statement of arrangements to the respondent.

103

This is known as "serving" the documents on the respondent. He or she will also receive two other documents from the court-the "acknowledgement of service" and the "notice of proceedings".

The notice of proceedings informs the respondent that divorce proceedings have been commenced against him or her and that person must acknowledge service within eight days. There are further instructions concerning seeking legal help or filling in acknowledgement personally.

This document, the acknowledgement of service, is self explanatory and is designed in question and answer form. It is designed to ensure the court that the respondent has received the papers and is fully aware of impending divorce proceedings against them. The court will not proceed with the case until it has received this information.

If you have commenced proceedings on the ground of adultery then the third party, who is known as the co-respondent is entitled to be notified of the divorce proceedings.

Non-defence of divorce proceedings

Where the respondent does not wish to defend proceedings, the next steps should be quite straightforward. The court will send either you or your solicitor a copy of the completed acknowledgement of service together with copies of two more forms known as "request for directions for trial (special procedure) and the "affidavit of evidence (special procedure) The special procedure indicates that the divorce process will be streamlined. Before, all petitioners seeking a divorce had to go to court and give evidence before a judge. This is no longer necessary. Like many county court procedures the route is now simplified and quicker.

The affidavit of evidence, like all affidavits, confirms that what you have said in your petition is true. You will need to "take an oath" in front of a solicitor which is called "swearing" the affidavit. Any questions concerning the truth later could ultimately, if it is discovered that you have lied, lead to contempt of court.

The "request for directions for trial" is a basic form requesting the court to proceed with your case. Both documents, the affidavit and the request for directions are then returned to court.

The case is then examined by an official of the court who will either declare that the facts of the case are proven, or otherwise.

If the district judge is happy with the case he or she will issue a certificate that you are entitled too a decree of divorce. Any claims for costs will also be considered at this stage.

When a certificate has been issued, a date will be fixed for decree nisi to be pronounced in open court by judge or district judge. You will be informed of this date but you need not attend court. However, if there is a dispute over costs you will need to attend and the matter will be dealt with by the judge

Both the respondent and petitioner are then sent a copy of the decree nisi by the court. However, you have not yet reached the stage of being finally divorced. It is only when your divorce has been made absolute at a later stage that you will be free to remarry if you wish. A decree absolute follows approximately six weeks after decree nisi.

If the district judge is not satisfied that you should be granted a divorce, then you will either be asked to produce further evidence or the matter will be sent for trial. This rarely happens.

You may be entitled to legal aid if this happens. This is dependent on your income and you should seek advice. If you are refused a divorce, and you have been handling the case yourself then you will most certainly need to go and see a solicitor.

Defence of divorce

If the respondent or co-respondent has returned the papers stating that he or she intends to defend the petition, your next move will be very much dependent on whether an "answer" setting out the defence has been filed. The respondent has 29 days to file a reply.

If a defence has been filed, then the special procedure designed to speed up the process can no longer be used. In this case it is advisable to see a solicitor. There will eventually be a date given for a hearing in court at which both the petitioner and respondent will be expected to attend.

Evidence will be given to the judge who will then have to decide if a divorce should be granted. Legal aid would almost certainly be available and the whole process, depending on the defence can be quite lengthy.

If you are the respondent and you feel that you wish to defend the petition you will almost certainly need to see a solicitor and take advice. In general, undefended straightforward cases, particularly where there are no children involved, can be done on a do-it-yourself basis. Anything more complicated will mean that you will probably need to see a solicitor.

If any other problems arise, such as the respondent either failing or refusing to return acknowledgement of service, proceedings will be delayed whilst a visit by a court official is made. This visit is to ascertain and provide evidence of service.

If the respondent cannot be traced, a request can be made to the court for the petition to be heard anyway. Again, this will result in delay.

11

Civil Partnerships Act 2004 And Civil Unions

A Civil partnership is a new legal relationship, which can be registered by two people of the same sex. Same-sex couples, within a civil partnership can obtain legal recognition for their relationship and can obtain the same benefits generally as married couples.

Civil partnership came into force on 5th December 2005. The first civil partnerships registered in England and Wales took place on 21st December 2005. Civil partners will be treated the same as married couples in many areas, including:

- Tax, including inheritance tax
- Employment benefits
- Most state and occupational pension benefits
- Income related benefits, tax credits and child support
- Maintenance for partner and children
- Ability to apply for parental responsibility for a civil partners child
- Inheritance of a tenancy agreement
- Recognition under intestacy rules
- Access to fatal accidents compensation
- Protection from domestic violence
- Recognition for immigration and nationality purposes

The registration of a civil partnership
Two people may register a civil partnership provided they are of the same sex, not already in a civil partnership or legally married, not closely related and both over 16 although consent of a parent or guardian must be obtained if either of them are under 18.

Registering a civil partnership is a secular procedure and is carried out by the registration service, which is responsible for the registration of births, deaths and marriages. A civil partnership registration is carried out under what is termed a standard procedure, which can be varied to take into account housebound people or people who are ill and are not expected to recover.

The standard procedure for registering a civil partnership

A couple wishing to register a civil partnership just have to decide the date they want to register and where they want the registration to take place. The formal process for registering consists of two main stages-the giving of a notice of intention to register and then the registration of the civil partnership itself.

The first stage, the giving of notice is a legal requirement and both partners have to do this at a register office in the area of a local authority where they live, even if they intend to register elsewhere. The notice contains the names, age, marital or civil partnership status, address, occupation, nationality and intended venue for the civil partnership. It is a criminal offence to give false information. If one of the partners is a non-EAA citizen and subject to immigration controls (see later) there are additional requirements to be fulfilled. Once the notice has been given it is displayed at the relevant register office for 15 days. This provided an opportunity for objections to be made. The civil partnership cannot be registered until after 15 clear days have elapsed from the date of the second person gives notice.

Each partner needs to give notice in the area that they have lived for at least seven days. If the couple live in different areas then each will post a notice in their own relevant area. When giving notice they will be asked where they wish the civil partnership to take place.

Residency requirements for a civil partnerships

A couple can register a civil partnership in England and Wales as long as they have both lived in a registration district in England and Wales for at least seven days immediately before giving notice. If one person lives in Scotland and the other lives in England or Wales, the person living in Scotland may give notice there. Officers, sailors or marines on board a

Royal Navy ship at sea can give notice to the captain or other commanding officer, providing they are going to register with someone who is resident in England and Wales. Service personnel based outside England and Wales have to fulfil the above residence requirements.

Documentary evidence of name, age and nationality will need to be shown. Passports and birth certificates are the main documents required. Proof of address will be required. If either partner has been married or in a civil partnership before evidence of divorce or dissolution will be required. If either partner is subject to immigration control a document showing entry clearance granted to form a civil partnership will need to be shown, along with a home office certificate of approval and indefinite leave to remain in the UK.

Changing names

After registering a civil partnership, one partner might want to change their surname to that of their partner. Government departments and agencies will accept civil partnership certificates as evidence for changing surnames.

Other private institutions may want a different form of evidence. It is up to the individual to check with the various organisations if they wish to change their surname.

Special circumstances

Variations to the standard procedure can be made in certain circumstances. If a partner is seriously ill and is not expected to recover then a civil partnership can be registered at any time. The 15-day waiting period will not apply. A certificate will need to be provided from a doctor stating that a person is not expected to recover and cannot be moved to a place where civil partnerships take place and that they understand the nature and purpose of signing the Registrar Generals licence.

Housebound people

If one partner is housebound there are special procedures to allow them to register a civil partnership at home.

A statement has to be signed, made by a doctor, confirming that this is the case and that the condition is likely to continue for the next three months. The statement must have been made no more than 14 days before notice being given and must be made on a standard form provided by the register office. The normal 15-day period will apply between giving notice and the civil partnership registration.

Detained people

There are special procedures to allow a couple to register a civil partnership at a place where one of them is detained in a hospital or prison. The couple has to provide a statement, made by the prison governor or responsible person confirming that the place where a person is detained can be named in the notice of proposed civil partnership as the place where the registration is to take place. This statement must have been made no more than 21 days prior to notice being given. The normal 15 day waiting period applies.

Gender change

The Gender Recognition Act 2004 enables transsexual people to change their legal gender by obtaining a full Gender Recognition Certificate. Where a transsexual person is married, they cannot obtain a full Gender Recognition Certificate without first ending their existing marriage. However, if they and their former spouse then wish to form a civil partnership with one another without delay, they can do so as soon as the full Gender Recognition Certificate has been issued. In those circumstances, they give notice and register on the same day.

More information is available about the process of changing gender on www.grp.gro.uk

Immigration requirements for people subject to immigration controls

The civil partnerships provisions for people subject to immigration control are exactly the same as those in place for marriage. These apply if one partner is a non-EAA (European Immigration Area) citizen and is subject to immigration control, for example in the UK on a visa.

Application for leave to remain

Civil partners of British citizens and people settled here can apply for an initial period of two years leave to remain in the UK. If they are still together at the end of that period they can apply for indefinite leave to remain.

A list of Register Offices for people subject to immigration control, can be found at www.ind.homeoffice.gov.uk or phone 0870 606 7766.

Overseas relationships

It may be the case that a couple has formed a civil union, registered partnership, domestic partnership or same-sex marriage abroad. Couples in those kind of relationships can automatically be recognised in the UK as civil partners without having to register again provided conditions set out in sections 212 to 218 of the Civil Partnership Act are met.

The legislation defines an overseas relationship that can be treated as a civil partnership ion the UK as one that is either specified in Schedule 20 to the Civil Partnership Act or one which meets general conditions in the Act and certain other conditions. Schedule 20 of the Act lists countries and relationships that are recognised. Countries listed in the Act are:

- Belgium
- Canada-Novia Scotia and Quebec
- Denmark
- Finland
- France
- Germany
- Iceland
- Netherlands
- Norway
- Sweden
- USA-Vermont

A couple who have formed a relationship recognised in one of those countries can be recognised in the UK as civil partners if they are of the same sex, the relationship has been registered with a responsible body in that country, the country were eligible to enter into a civil relationship in that country and all procedural requirements have been fulfilled.

For foreign relationships in countries not listed in Schedule 20 a couple who have formed a relationship can still be recognised as civil partners if the foreign relationship meets the general conditions set out in the Civil Partnerships Act.

To find out which foreign relationships are contained within Schedule 20, which is revised periodically, go to www.womenandequalityunit.gov.uk/civilpartnership.htm

Family relationships
The law now recognises the role of both civil partners in respect of a child living in their household.

Adoption
Under the Adoption and Children Act 2002, which came into force on 30th December 2005, civil partners may apply jointly to adopt a child.

Parental responsibility
Under the Adoption and Children Act 2002, a person will also be able to acquire parental responsibility for the child of their civil partner. They can do this with the agreement of their civil partner. If the child's other parent also has parental responsibility, both parents must agree. Parental responsibility can also be acquired on application to the court. Civil partners will have a duty to provide maintenance for each other and any children of the civil partnership.

Social security, tax credits and child support
Entering into a civil partnership will affect entitlements to the benefits and tax credits a person may be receiving. For a list of benefits and other advice contact the Benefit Enquiry Line on 0800 882200.

Tax credits

From 5th December the income of a civil partner has been taken into account when calculating entitlement to child and working tax credits. The Tax Credit Line on 0845 300 3900 can offer further advice.

Child support

From 5th December 2005, civil partners who are parents will be treated in the same way as married partners for Child Support. Also, parents who are living with a same sex partner even where they have not formed a civil partnership will be treated in the same way as parents who live together with an opposite sex partner but who are not married. For further information contact the Child Support Agency on 08457 133133.

Pensions

Survivor benefits in occupational and personal pension schemes. Surviving civil partners will be entitled to a pension based on accrued pension right. New rules for civil partners mean that a surviving partner will benefit from a survivors pension based on the contracted out pension rights accrued by their deceased partner from 1988 to the date of retirement or death if this occurs before retirement. This new rule applies to all contracted out private pension schemes.

State pensions

From 5th December 2005, civil partners have enjoyed most of the same state pension rights as husbands and they will treated the same as husbands and wives after 2010 when the treatment of men and women will be equalised. For more information concerning pensions contact the Pension Service on 0845 6060625.

Tax

From 5th December 2005, civil partners have been treated the same as married couples for tax purposes. Information is available from a local tax office and the HMRC website www.hmrc.gov.uk

Employment rights

Employers are required to treat both married partners and civil partners in the same way. The Employment Equality (Sexual Orientation) Regulations 2003 have been amended to ensure that civil partners receive the same treatment and can bring a claim for sexual orientation discrimination if this is not the case. Other areas where changes are made include flexible working, where a civil partner of a child under six or disabled child under 18 will be able to take advantage of flexible working arrangements. Paternity and adoption leave will now be the right of civil partners More information on paternity and adoption leave and pay can be found on www.dti.gov.uk/workingparents.

Tenancy rights

The general effect of the Civil Partnerships act has been to give the same rights to civil partners as married couples. The Act also equalises the rights of same sex couples who are living together as if they were civil partners and their families with those of unmarried opposite sex couples.

Private sector tenants

The same sex partner of an assured tenant or assured shorthold tenant will have the same rights of succession to a tenancy as those tenants of local authority or registered social landlords. For further information on housing and tenancies visit www.odpm.gov.uk
. You can also e mail and enquiry to the Office of the deputy prime Minister on enquiryodpm@odpm.gsi.gov.uk

Dissolution of a civil partnership

A civil partnership ends only on the death of one of the civil partners, or on the dissolution of the partnership or a nullity odder or a presumption of death order by the court.

The usual route is for one of the partners to seek a dissolution order to terminate the civil partnership. Other options are available. If one party, for example, did not validly consent as a result of duress, mistake or unsoundness of mind, then a nullity order may be sought from the court. Or of both civil partners do not wish to terminate the partnership one f them may ask the court for a separation order.

The dissolution process

Whoever decides to end the civil partnership should seek legal advice. The case will usually be dealt with by a civil partnership proceedings county court, although complex cases will be referred to the high court.

To end a civil partnership the applicant (petitioner) must prove to the court that the civil partnership has irretrievably broken down. Proof of an irretrievable breakdown is based on the following:

- Unreasonable behaviour by both other civil partner
- Separation for two years with the consent of the other civil partner
- Separation for five years without the consent of the other civil partner
- If the other civil partner has deserted the applicant for a period of two years or more.

Nullity

In exceptional circumstances one party to a civil partnership may decide to seek a court order (a 'Nullity' order) to annul the civil partnership.

Separation

The grounds on which a separation order may be sought are exactly the same as those for a dissolution order. Te end result is different, as a person whose civil partnership has been dissolved is free to marry or form a new partnership whereas a person who has separated remains a civil partner.

Property and financial arrangements

If a civil partnership is ending or if the couple are separating, they will need to decide what happens to any property belonging to them. If they agree on a division they can ask the court to approve the agreement. If they cannot agree they can ask the court to decide. The court has power to make a range of orders in relation to property and other assets including income:

- The court can make an order that one civil partner pay maintenance to the other either for the benefit of the civil partner or for the benefit of any children of the relationship. These orders are known as financial provision orders.

115

- The court can make an order which will adjust the property rights of the civil partners as regards to property and other assets which they own, either together or separately. This may, for example, mean ordering the transfer and ownership of property from one civil partner to another for that persons benefit or the benefit of any children (known as property adjustment orders)
- The court can make an order in relation to the future pension entitlement of one of the civil partners in favour of the other. This order can relate to occupational pensions, personal pensions and other annuities (known as pension sharing orders)

Financial provision orders for maintenance can be made before a civil partnership has been ended or as separation order granted by the court. Property adjustment and pension sharing orders only take legal effect once dissolution, separation or nullity order has been made by the court. Even if the couple have been able to agree on maintenance and other property issues they should seek professional advice on such issued. In most cases the solicitor dealing with the end of the civil partnership will be able to provide appropriate advice. If you require details of local solicitors with experience in this are you should go to www.clsdirect.org.uk/index.isp or phone the community legal service on 0845 3454345.

Care of children

Agreeing arrangements for the care of any children should be the first priority of couples who are ending their civil partnerships or choosing to live apart through separation. If a couple decide to end the civil [partnership the court will want to ensure that both partners are happy with the arrangements for looking after children. If a couple are unable to agree the court will decide for them, or may do so, as part of the dissolution proceedings.

12

THE LAW AND NEIGHBOURS

The majority of people live peaceably with their neighbours. In fact, good relations with neighbours is essential for the maintenance of a healthy and balanced community. However, it is also the case that, at times, relations with neighbours break down and people turn to the law to obtain justice.

It is an unfortunate fact, particularly in the large urban centres, such as London, that people can live for years in a street and not know their neighbours. People become landlords and let their properties, which can lead to disruption if the incoming tenants are anti-social and do not have strong ties to an area.

The law strikes a balance when dealing with neighbour disputes. On one hand, people are free to use their property as they wish. On the other, it is essential that the rights of others are respected when we decide to embark on a course of action in our own property.

There are specialist organisations, based on mediation, who try to resolve disputes without recourse to the law. These organisations are usually within local authority areas, are free and can resolve disputes through mediating with the parties involved. See useful addresses for addresses of mediators.

In law, we both have a 'duty of care' and a duty to be reasonable to our neighbours. Essentially, this duty is to treat a person or people with the same degree of care and respect that we would expect to be afforded. It is when this is not the case that the law comes into play.

Neighbours and noise complaints
Of all the complaints that neighbours level against each other, the most common is that of noise. Noise can arise from many different sources, crying babies, footsteps and general movement, parties, dogs and so on.

117

In each case, the law would recognise a reasonable level, over which legal action is seen to be reasonable. Generally, the local environmental health department of the council would provide measurements of noise and would determine what is reasonable. One main problem that has arisen is that of inadequate sound proofing, particularly in converted flats and new build properties. Builders have tended to construct properties with a minimum level of soundproofing that has proved to be inadequate.

In all disputes with neighbours, resorting to the law should be the last course of action. There are a number of other alternatives to consider first. It is always best to try to solve problems amicably. In the long run this proves the most fruitful as you will likely be neighbours for a long time to come and you will want to maintain good relationships.

The first thing to do is to talk to your neighbours and to establish what the nature of the problem is and whether your neighbours can acknowledge that there is a problem and do something about it. It might also help to speak to other neighbours and see whether they are also affected in the same way.

It is advisable to keep written records of the noise, a diary of sorts, recording the nature and type of noise and the frequency. This is the only way to create a tangible body of evidence.

Contacting landlords

If you feel that you cannot solve the problem by approaching the people concerned then it may be necessary to contact a landlord. The nature of a landlord can have a bearing on a person's ability to solve a case, whether the landlord is a social landlord, i.e. a housing association or local authority or private landlord. In many cases, the person creating the noise will also be an owner-occupier.

Social landlords

If the landlord of a person or people creating a noise is a social landlord, i.e. a housing association or local authority, the first thing that you should do, having tried to solve the problem amicably and started to keep a diary, is to contact the landlord and lodge a complaint, making it clear that you are maintaining a diary. The landlord will have signed a tenancy with the person involved and part of that tenancy agreement will be a covenant that the tenant does not cause a nuisance or annoyance to his/her neighbours. The landlord will contact the tenant and will begin the process whereby, ultimately; the tenant could be evicted for breach of tenancy. However, it is important to realise that taking such action successfully can be a long and difficult process and it may be easier to take your own action, or at least take your own action in conjunction with the landlord.

Environmental Health Departments

The 1990 Environmental Protection Act (EPA) is the guiding framework within which environmental health officers operate. An individual can go direct to the Environmental Health Department, as can a landlord. In addition, the Environmental Health Department can also take action against individuals without waiting for a complaint to come in. To compliment environmental health, a landlord, particularly social landlords, can use independent witnesses to back up other bodies. Some local authorities operate 'noise patrols' which are intended to back up other evidence.

The EHO (Environmental Health Officer) will usually write a letter to the offending person, which will serve as a warning. If this does not work, then the EHO will write a letter stating that the individual is in breach of Section 80 of the EPA and, if the noise is not abated then the matter can become a criminal offence with a fine and/or prison sentence attached to it.

Using the Magistrates Court

There are other alternatives to the Environmental Health Department. A person suffering noise nuisance can go to the Magistrates court, under section 82 of the Environmental Protection Act 1990. Before you do so you have to give your neighbour formal written warning of your intention to take the matter to the magistrate's court, and this may well be sufficient to stop the noise. If it does not, then you have to fill in the appropriate forms, which can be obtained from the magistrates court, and make an appointment for a hearing.

119

The court will need to be satisfied that a genuine noise nuisance exists and that you have made an effort to solve it directly with your neighbour. If they are satisfied then they will issue a 'noise abatement order' and it becomes a criminal offence to breach this order.

Using the county court

Going to the county court is another alternative. You could begin a civil action in a county court to obtain an injunction to stop noise. The complaint must, however, be serious and the noise intolerable to obtain an injunction. Injunctions are expensive and difficult to obtain and the burden of proof that much greater. If you are attempting to obtain an injunction then you will almost certainly need a solicitor.

Owner-occupiers and noise

If you own your own property and the person causing the nuisance is also an owner-occupier them you will not have a landlord to complain to, unless the person is a leaseholder. If the person is a leaseholder then you should establish who the freeholder is, i.e. who built and sold the property and insist that this person takes action under the lease. In addition to this, you should complain to the Environmental health officer of the Local Authority or go to the magistrate's court in order to attempt to stop the noise.

If the person is a freeholder, and there is no landlord then you can only pursue the remedies described, i.e. EHO or magistrates court.

You could try contacting the police. However, unless the problem is domestic violence or some other criminal offence, the police are reluctant to get involved.

Other sources of noise

There are many sources of noise, in particular street noise, that cannot be pinpointed to a neighbour but nevertheless cause distress to others. One such source of noise is that of car alarms. In addition, builders and others operating in the streets can also cause noise nuisance. In order to combat the problems of street noise, a Noise and Statutory Nuisance Act came into effect in 1994 and extends the scope of the Environmental Protection Act 1990, so that street noise is also classified as a statutory nuisance.

The Act covers nuisance from vehicles, machinery or equipment in the street. It deals in particular with car alarms and burglar alarms. The concept of 'street' covers not only roads but also pathways, square or court open to the public. It does not mater whether the area is private or public. 'Equipment' includes musical equipment and even ice cream vans and buskers.

The exclusions
The Act does not apply to traffic noise, political demonstrations or noise made by any 'naval, military or air force'.

Car alarms
The person responsible for a car with a faulty alarm is the person who is the registered owner of the vehicle, or any other person who, for the time being, is responsible for the vehicle. An Environmental Health Officer can serve an abatement notice on that person to remedy the fault. The EHO can serve a notice on the vehicle and, if after an hour nothing further has been done or the person responsible has not been found, the EHO can either immobilise the alarm or remove the vehicle. The EHO has powers to open and enter a car, causing as little damage as possible. It must also be secured against theft when the EHO has completed the task.

House alarms
Householders have to inform local authorities of alarms that they intend to install. The alarm must meet prescribed requirements and the police must be informed of any key holders and of their telephone numbers. If any alarm is still operating one hour after it has been set off, then an officer of the local authority can enter and turn off that alarm providing that he or she has permission to do so. If no permission from the owner is forthcoming then a warrant can be obtained from a justice of the peace to enter the premises, if necessary by force, as long as damage is kept to a minimum and the premises is secured.

The owner can be called upon to reimburse the authority for any cost incurred.

121

Problems with boundaries and fences

There is no absolute rule of law that requires a person to mark a boundary of his or her property or to enclose it with a fence. However, even if there are no rules, it is always advisable to reach agreement with neighbours about boundaries. If you are buying a property, always try to ensure that the boundaries are clearly marked and that it is clear what land you will own. Ascertain rights of way and car parking, if appropriate. Be very wary of buying a property where the plan does not tally with what you actually see on the ground. If in doubt contact the boundary skills panel of the Royal Institution of Chartered Surveyors (see useful addresses).

Plans

In general, with any conveyance of land there should be a plan. annexed to the title deeds, which is supposed to show where the boundaries to a property lie. However, a plan can be inaccurate, misleading or out of date. If you have not established the boundaries before you move in and trouble arises from a neighbour, the question is, what is the remedy?

The objective test

In general, the court will take an objective view, i.e. what are the facts? The court will look at the plan but will also look at all the surrounding circumstances that have resulted in the situation arising. On many occasions, there will be a trip arranged to the disputed are in order to ascertain the nature of the problem.

Fences

Even where there is no demarcation dispute between neighbours a frequent source of tension can be responsibility for the upkeep of fences. Who owns the fence and who should keep it in repair?

General rules regarding ownership

There are certain assumptions about responsibility for fences. Generally, where title deeds do have a plan then that plan will demark any fence ownership and if the 'T' mark used to demark the fence falls on your side then you will be responsible.

No 'T' marks or no plan

If there is no 'T'mark or no plan then there is a general assumption that you own the fence if the supporting posts are on your land.

Party fences

You can decide to have a party fence with both sides owning the fence and both sides contributing to the costs of repair. This is usually prevalent where ownership cannot be ascertained. Part wall legislation will generally find that both parties are responsible for the upkeep.

Mending fences

In general, if a fence belongs to a neighbour he or she is not under a legal duty to repair it. You can only insist on repair if it represents a hazard to your land and property. In this case, you can approach an environmental health officer and lodge a complaint under the Environmental Health Act. If you need to repair the fence at your own expense because it is a danger, you will need your neighbour's permission to go on to his/her land, otherwise you are trespassing. Otherwise, you would have to go to court for leave to go onto the land.

Party walls

In theory, a neighbour on each side of a party wall owns half the wall, whether the division is made vertically or horizontally. Where two buildings have been standing for 20 years or more, each neighbour acquires a right, called an easement, against the neighbour on the other side for the right of support to their property.

General duty to take care

It is reasonable for the law to impose a duty to take care on the owner of a party wall, so that whether he uses it, removes it, builds on it, or repairs it he must minimise the possibility of damage to neighbouring property. In addition, allowing a party wall to fall into disrepair can cause a nuisance and an adjoining owner can sue for damages.

Problems with nuisance generally

There are three types of nuisances, or categories of nuisance in law:

- private nuisance
- public nuisance
- statutory nuisance

Private nuisance

A private nuisance has been defined as something that occurs on someone else's property, which detrimentally affects your property or your enjoyment of your own property. Equally, something that happens on your property can be a source of nuisance to your neighbour. As we have discussed, the first course of action to be taken when dealing with private nuisance is that of approaching your neighbour and trying to find a remedy. Only then should there be recourse to the law. The Environmental Protection Act 1990 is the Act that regulates nuisance. However, with private nuisance, Environmental Health officers are reluctant to get involved unless the nuisance is prolonged and severe.

Public nuisance

A public nuisance is something that detrimentally affects a large group of people and not only an individual. It often concerns obstructions on the highways.

Statutory nuisance

Certain types of nuisance are covered by legislation. In particular, the Environmental protection Act 1990 has laid down various matters associated with property. As the name of the Act suggests, the law is primarily concerned with those who use their property in such a way as to cause a potential health hazard. The Act refers to the state of the premises, smoke, fumes, dust and any accumulation or deposit of substances that could be prejudicial to health or could cause a nuisance.

It is the well being of the population as a whole that the Act is concerned with. However, you can use its provisions for the protection of your own well being by notifying your local authority of apparent breaches.

The local authority has to take steps to remedy a breach, by investigating a complaint and warning a perpetrator if there is cause to do so. If the matter has to be taken further then the Act provides for a series of steps that ultimately lead to criminal action and a fine or imprisonment if found guilty.

Problems with gardens

Overhanging plants and trees

The general rule is that you are entitled to your own space, in and above (to some extent) your own property. So branches from neighbours trees or shrubs which overhang your garden are intrusions into your space, therefore they can be regarded as trespass and nuisance. You are entitled to lop off branches which intrude over your side of the fence. You are supposed to return the branches to your neighbour (and any growth such as fruit).

However, in these cases, it is better to negotiate with your neighbour before taking action. If you need to gain access to someone else's property to deal with tress and shrubs then you have the right to apply to court under the Access to Neighbouring Land Act 1992 to allow you to solve the problem.

Obviously, this is extreme and is usually done where the landlord cannot be found or identified.

The same rules apply to roots that are growing into your property and are causing damage. You can cap those roots, as long as the tree is not damaged or you can apply to court for an injunction to prevent any further growth and also sue for damages.

13

THE LAW AND LANDLORD AND TENANT

Explaining the law

As a landlord or tenant it is very important to understand rights and obligations, exactly what can and what cannot be done once the tenancy agreement has been signed and the tenant has moved into the property. Some landlords think they can do exactly as they please, because the property belongs to them. Some tenants do not know any differently and therefore the landlord can, and often does, get away with breaking the law. However, it is important that you have a grasp on the key principles of the law. In order to fully understand the law we should begin by looking at the main types of relationship between people and their homes.

The freehold and the lease

In law, there are two main types of ownership and occupation of property. These are: freehold and leasehold. These arrangements are very old indeed.

Freehold

If a person owns their property outright (usually with a mortgage) then they are a freeholder. The only claims to ownership over and above their own might be those of the building society or the bank, which lent them the money to buy the place. They will re-possess the property if the mortgage payments are not kept up with. In certain situations though, the local authority (council) for an area can affect a person's right to do what they please with their home even if they are a freeholder. This will occur when planning powers are exercised, for example, in order to prevent the carrying out of alterations without consent.

The local authority for your area has many powers and we will be referring to these regularly in each Chapter of this Guide.

Leasehold

If a person lives in a property owned by someone else and has a written agreement allowing them to occupy the flat or house for a period of time i.e., giving them permission to live in that property, then they will, in the main, have a lease and either be a leaseholder or a tenant of a landlord.

The main principle of a lease is that a person has been given permission by someone else to live in his or her property for a period of time. The person giving permission could be either the freeholder or another leaseholder.

The tenancy agreement is one type of lease. If you have issued a tenancy agreement then you will have given permission to a person live in your property for a period of time.

The position of the tenant

The tenant will usually have an agreement for a shorter period of time than the typical leaseholder. Whereas the leaseholder will, for example, have an agreement for ninety-nine years, the tenant will have an agreement, which either runs from week to week or month to month (periodic tenancy) or is for a fixed term, for example, one-year.

These arrangements are the most common types of agreement between the private landlord and tenant.

The agreement itself will state whether it is a fixed term or periodic tenancy. If an agreement has not been issued it will be assumed to be a periodic tenancy.

Both periodic and fixed term tenants will usually pay a sum of rent regularly to a landlord in return for permission to live in the property (more about rent and service charges later)

The tenancy agreement

The tenancy agreement is the usual arrangement under which one person will live in a property owned by another. Before a tenant moves into a property he/she will have to sign a tenancy agreement drawn up by a landlord or landlord's agent. *A tenancy agreement is a contract between landlord and tenant.*

127

It is important to realize that when you sign a tenancy agreement, you have signed a contract with another person, which governs the way in which they will live in their property.

The contract

Typically, any tenancy agreement will show the name and address of the landlord and will state the names of the tenant(s). The type of tenancy agreement that is signed should be clearly indicated. This could be, for example, a Rent Act protected tenancy, an assured tenancy or an assured shorthold tenancy. In the main, the agreement will be an assured shorthold.

The date the tenancy began and the duration (fixed term or periodic) plus the amount of rent payable should be clearly shown, along with who is responsible for any other charges, such as water rates, council tax etc, and a description of the property you are renting out.

In addition to the rent that must be paid there should be a clear indication of when a rent increase can be expected. This information is sometimes shown in other conditions of tenancy, which should be given to the tenant when they move into their home. The conditions of tenancy will set out landlords and tenants rights and obligations.

If services are provided, i.e., if a service charge is payable, this should be indicated in the agreement. The tenancy agreement should indicate clearly the address to which notices on the landlord can be served by the tenant, for example, because of repair problems or notice of leaving the property. The landlord has a legal requirement to indicate this.

The tenancy agreement will either be a basic document with the above information or will be more comprehensive. Either way, there will be a section beginning "the tenant agrees." Here the tenant will agree to move into the property, pay rent, use the property as an only home, not cause a nuisance to others, take responsibility for certain internal repairs, not sublet the property, i.e., create another tenancy, and various other things depending on the property.

There should also be another section "the landlord agrees". Here, the landlord is contracting with the tenant to allow quiet enjoyment of the property. The landlord's repairing responsibilities are also usually outlined.

Finally, there should be a section entitled "ending the tenancy" which will outline the ways in which landlord and tenant can end the agreement. It is in this section that the landlord should make reference to the "grounds for possession". Grounds for possession are circumstances where the landlord will apply to court for possession of his/her property. Some of these grounds relate to what is in the tenancy, i.e., the responsibility to pay rent and to not cause a nuisance.

Other grounds do not relate to the contents of the tenancy directly, but more to the law governing that particular tenancy. The grounds for possession are very important, as they are used in any court case brought against the tenant. Unfortunately, they are not always indicated in the tenancy agreement. As they are so important they are summarized later on in this chapter.

It must be said at this point that many residential tenancies are very light on landlord's responsibilities. Repairing responsibilities, and responsibilities relating to rental payment, are landlords obligations under law. This book deals with these, and other areas. However, many landlords will seek to use only the most basic document in order to conceal legal obligations.

The public sector tenancy (local authority or housing association), for example, is usually very clear and very comprehensive about the rights and obligations of landlord and tenant. Unfortunately, the private landlord often does not employ the same energy when it comes to educating and informing the tenant. This is one of the main reasons for this book. It is essential that those who intend to let property for profit are able to manage professionally and set high standards as a private landlord. This is because the sector has been beset by rogues in the past.

The responsibility to provide a tenant with a rent book

If the tenant is a weekly periodic tenant the landlord must provide him/her with a rent book and commits a criminal offence if he/she does not do so. This is outlined in the Landlord and Tenant Act 1985 sections 4 - 7. Under this Act any tenant can ask in writing the name and address of the landlord. The landlord must reply within twenty-one days of asking.

129

As most tenancies nowadays are fixed term assured shortholds then it is not strictly necessary to provide a tenant with a rent book. However, for the purposes of business efficiency, and your own records, it is always useful to issue a rent book to tenants and sign it each time rent is collected or a standing order is paid.

Overcrowding and the rules governing too many people living in the property

It is important to understand, when signing a tenancy agreement, that it is not permitted to allow the premises to become overcrowded, i.e., to allow more people than was originally intended, (which is outlined in the agreement) to live in the property! If a tenant does then the landlord can take action to evict.

Different types of tenancy agreement

The protected tenancy - the meaning of the term

As a basic guide, if a person is a private tenant and signed their current agreement with a landlord before 15th January 1989 then they will, in most cases, be a protected tenant with all the rights relating to protection of tenure, which are considerable. Protection is provided under the 1977 Rent Act.

In practice, there are not many protected tenancies left and the investor will usually be managing an assured shorthold tenancy.

The assured shorthold tenancy - what it means

If the tenant entered into an agreement with a landlord after 15th January 1989 then they will, in most cases, be an assured tenant. We will discuss assured tenancies in more depth in chapter seven. In brief, there are various types of assured tenancy. The assured shorthold is usually a fixed term version of the assured tenancy and enables the landlord to recover their property after six months and to vary the rent after this time.

At this point it is important to understand that the main difference between the two types of tenancy, protected and assured, is that the tenant has less rights as a tenant under the assured tenancy. For example, they will not be entitled, as is a protected tenant, to a fair rent set by a Rent Officer.

Other types of agreement

In addition to the above tenancy agreements, there are other types of agreement sometimes used in privately rented property. One of these is the company let, as we discussed in the last chapter, and another is the license agreement. The person signing such an agreement is called a licensee.

Licenses will only apply in special circumstances where the licensee cannot be given sole occupation of his home and therefore can only stay for a short period with minimum rights. It is not the intention to pursue licensees further in this book.

The squatter (trespasser)

In addition to the tenant and licensee, there is one other type of occupation of property, which needs mentioning. This is squatting. It is useful for the would-be landlord to have a basic understanding of this are of occupation.

The squatter is usually someone who has gained entry to a vacant property, either a house or a flat, without permission.

Although the squatter, a trespasser, has the protection of the law and cannot be evicted without a court order, if he or she is to be given the protection of the law, the squatted property must have been empty in the first place.

On gaining entry to a property, the squatter will normally put up a notice claiming squatter's rights, which means that they are identifying themselves as a person or group having legal protection until a court order is obtained to evict them. Even if no notice is visible, the squatter has protection and it is an offence to attempt to remove them forcibly.

The squatter has protection from eviction under the Protection from Eviction Act 1977 and is also protected from violence or harassment by the Criminal Law Act of 1977.

The trespasser who has entered an occupied property without permission has fewer rights. Usually, the police will either arrest or escort a trespasser off the premises. There is no protection from eviction. However, there is protection from violence and intimidation under the Protection from Harassment Act of 1977.

The assured tenant

All tenancies, with the exceptions detailed entered into after 15th January 1989, are known as assured tenancies. An assured shorthold, which is the most common form of tenancy used by the landlord nowadays, is one type of assured tenancy, and is for a fixed term of six months minimum and can be brought to an end with two months notice by serving a section 21 (of the Housing Act 1988) notice.

Assured tenancies are governed by the 1988 Housing Act, as amended by the 1996 Housing Act. It is to these Acts, or outlines of the Acts that the landlord must refer when intending to sign a tenancy and let a residential property.

For a tenancy to be assured, three conditions must be fulfilled:

1. The premises must be a dwelling house. This basically means any premises, which can be lived in. Business premises will normally fall outside this interpretation.
2. There must exist a particular relationship between landlord and tenant. In other words there must exist a tenancy agreement. For example, a licence to occupy, as in the case of students, or accommodation occupied as a result of work, cannot be seen as a tenancy. Following on from this, the accommodation must be let as a single unit. The tenant, who must be an individual, must normally be able to sleep, cook and eat in the accommodation. Sharing of bathroom facilities will not prevent a tenancy being an assured tenancy but shared cooking or other facilities, such as a living room, will.
3. The third requirement for an assured tenancy is that the tenant must occupy the dwelling as his or her only or principal home. In situations involving joint tenants at least one of them must occupy.

Tenancies that are not assured

A tenancy agreement will not be assured if one of the following conditions applies:

-The tenancy or the contract was entered into before 15th January 1989;

-If no rent is payable or if only a low rent amounting to less than two thirds of the present ratable value of the property is payable;

-If the premises are let for business purposes or for mixed residential and business purposes;

-If part of the dwelling house is licensed for the sale of liquor for consumption on the premises. This does not include the publican who lets out a flat;

-If the dwelling house is let with more than two acres of agricultural land;

-If the dwelling house is part of an agricultural holding and is occupied in relation to carrying out work on the holding;

-If the premises are let by a specified institution to students, i.e., halls of residence;

-If the premises are let for the purpose of a holiday;

-Where there is a resident landlord, e.g., in the case where the landlord has let one of his rooms but continues to live in the house;

-If the landlord is the Crown (the monarchy) or a government department. Certain lettings by the Crown are capable of being assured, such as some lettings by the Crown Estate Commissioners;

-If the landlord is a local authority, a fully mutual housing association (this is where you have to be a shareholder to be a tenant) a newly created Housing Action Trust or any similar body listed in the 1988 Housing Act.

-If the letting is transitional such as a tenancy continuing in its original form until phased out, such as:

-A protected tenancy under the 1977 Rent Act;

-Secure tenancy granted before 1st January 1989, e.g., from a local authority or housing association. These tenancies are governed by the 1985 Housing Act).

The Assured Shorthold tenancy

The assured shorthold tenancy as we have seen, is the most common form of tenancy used in the private sector. The main principle of the assured shorthold tenancy is that it is issued for a period of six months minimum and can be brought to an end by the landlord serving two months notice on the tenant. At the end of the six-month period the tenant, if given two months prior notice, must leave.

Any property let on an assured tenancy can be let on an assured shorthold, providing the following three conditions are met:

- The tenancy must be for a fixed term of not less than six months.
- The agreement cannot contain powers, which enable the landlord to end the tenancy before six months. This does not include the right of the landlord to enforce the grounds for possession, which will be approximately the same as those for the assured tenancy
- A notice requiring possession at the end of the term is usually served two months before that date.
- A notice must be served before any rent increase giving one months clear notice and providing details of the rent increase.

If the landlord wishes to get possession of his/her property, in this case before the expiry of the contractual term, the landlord has to gain a court order. A notice of seeking possession must be served, giving fourteen days notice and following similar grounds of possession as an assured tenancy.

The landlord cannot simply tell a tenant to leave before the end of the agreed term.

A copy of a notice of seeking possession for an assured shorthold tenancy is shown in the Appendix.

If the tenancy runs on after the end of the fixed term then the landlord can regain possession by giving the required two months notice, as mentioned above.

At the end of the term for which the assured shorthold tenancy has been granted, the landlord has an automatic right to possession.

An assured shorthold tenancy will become periodic (will run from week to week) when the initial term of six months has elapsed and the landlord has not brought the tenancy to an end.

Assured shorthold tenants, can be evicted only on certain grounds some discretionary, some mandatory (see below).

In order for the landlord of an assured shorthold tenant to regain possession of the property, a notice of seeking possession (of property) must be served, giving fourteen days notice of expiry and stating the ground for possession. A copy of this notice is shown in Appendix 3. This notice is similar to a notice to quit, discussed in the previous chapter.

Following the fourteen days a court order must be obtained. Although gaining a court order is not complicated, a solicitor will usually be used. Court costs can be awarded against the tenant.

Security of tenure: The ways in which a tenant can lose their home as an assured shorthold tenant

There are a number of circumstances called grounds (mandatory and discretionary) whereby a landlord can start a court action to evict a tenant.

These are *mandatory* grounds (where the judge must give the landlord possession) and *discretionary* grounds (where the judge does not have to give the landlord possession) on which a court can order possession if the home is subject to an assured tenancy.

The grounds cover such things as non-payment of rent and nuisance. A full copy of the grounds can be found in the 1988 Housing Act. A copy can be obtained from your local library, or a digest of the grounds can be found on the internet.

Fast track possession

In November 1993, following changes to the County Court Rules, a facility was introduced which enables landlords of tenants with assured shorthold tenancies to apply for possession of their property without the usual time delay involved in waiting for a court date and attendance at court. This is known as "fast track possession" It cannot be used for rent arrears or other grounds. It is used to gain possession of a property when the fixed term of six months or more has come to an end and the tenant will not move.

If the landlord wishes to raise rent, at least one month's minimum notice must be given. The rent cannot be raised more than once for the same tenant in one year. Tenants have the right to challenge a rent increase if they think it is unfair by referring the rent to a Rent Assessment Committee. The committee will prevent the landlord from raising the rent above the ordinary market rent for that type of property.

Joint Tenancies

Joint tenancies: the position of two or more people who have a tenancy agreement for one property

Although it is the normal state of affairs for a tenancy agreement, to be granted to one person, this is not always the case.

A tenancy can also be granted to two or more people and is then known as a *joint tenancy*. The position of joint tenants is exactly the same as that of single tenants. In other words, there is still one tenancy even though it is shared.

Each tenant is responsible for paying the rent and observing the terms and conditions of the tenancy agreement. No one joint tenant can prevent another joint tenants access to the premises.

If one of the joint tenants dies then his or her interest will automatically pass to the remaining joint tenants. A joint tenant cannot dispose of his or her interest in a will. If one joint tenant, however, serves a notice to quit (notice to leave the property) on another joint tenant(s) then the tenancy will come to an end and the landlord can apply to court for a possession order, if the remaining tenant does not leave.

The position of a wife or husband in relation to joint tenancies is rather more complex because the married person has more rights when it comes to the home than the single person.

Remember: the position of a tenant who has signed a joint tenancy agreement is exactly the same as that of the single tenant. If one person leaves, the other(s) have the responsibilities of the tenancy. If one person leaves without paying his share of the rent then the other tenants will have to pay instead.

Rent
The payment of rent and other financial matters
If a tenancy is protected under the Rent Act 1977, as described earlier there is the right to apply to the Rent Officer for the setting of a fair rent for the property.

The assured tenant and rent
The assured (shorthold) tenant has far fewer rights in relation to rent control than the protected tenant.

The Housing Act 1988 allows a landlord to charge whatever he likes. There is no right to a fair or reasonable rent with an assured tenancy. The rent can sometimes be negotiated at the outset of the tenancy. This rent has to be paid as long as the contractual term of the tenancy lasts. Once the contractual term has expired, the landlord is entitled to continue to charge the same rent.

On expiry of an assured shorthold the landlord is free to grant a new tenancy and set the rent to a level that is compatible with the market.

Rent control for assured shorthold tenants
We have seen that the assured shorthold tenancy is for a period of six months minimum. Like the assured tenant, the assured shorthold tenant

has no right to request that a fair rent should be set. The rent is a market rent. As with an assured tenancy, the assured shorthold tenant has the right to appeal to a Rent Assessment Committee in the case of what he/she considers an unreasonable rent. This may be done during the contractual term of the tenancy. The Committee will consider whether the rent is significantly higher than is usual for a similar property.

If the Committee assesses a different rent from that set by the landlord, they may set a date when the increase will take effect. The rent cannot be backdated to before the date of the application. Once a decision has been reached by the Committee, the landlord cannot increase the rent for at least twelve months, or on termination of the tenancy.

Council tax and the tenant

From April 1993 the council tax replaced the poll tax. Unlike poll tax, the council tax is based on properties, or dwellings, and not individual people.

This means that there is one bill for each individual dwelling, rather than separate bills for each person. The number and type of people who live in the dwelling may affect the size of the final bill. A discount of 25% is given for people who live alone. Each property is placed in a valuation band with different properties paying more or less depending on their individual value. Tenants who feel that their home has been placed in the wrong valuation band can appeal to their local authority council tax department.

Who has to pay the council tax?

In most cases the tenant occupying the dwelling will have to pay the council tax. However, a landlord will be responsible for paying the council tax where there are several households living in one dwelling.

This will usually be hostels, bedsits and other non-self contained flats where people share things such as cooking and washing facilities. The council tax on this type of property remains the responsibility of the landlord even if all but one of the tenants move out.

Although the landlord has the responsibility for paying the council tax, he or she will normally try to pass on the increased cost through rents. However, there is a set procedure for a landlord to follow if he/she wishes to increase rent.

Dwellings, which are exempt

Certain properties will be exempt from the council tax, such as student's halls of residences and nurse's homes. Properties with all students resident will be exempt from the tax. However, if one non-student moves in then that property will no longer be exempt from tax. Uninhabitable empty properties are exempt from tax, as they are not counted as dwellings. This is not the same as homes, which have been declared as unfit for human habitation by Environmental Health officers. The deciding factor will be whether or not a property is capable of being lived in.

Reductions in council tax bills

Tenants in self-contained accommodation who live alone will be entitled to a discount of 25% of the total bill. Tenants may also qualify for the discount if they share their homes with people who do not count for council tax purposes. Such people are: children under eighteen; students; patients resident in hospital; people who are severely mentally impaired; low paid careworkers; eighteen or nineteen year olds still at school (or just left); people in prison (except for non-payment of fines or the council tax); and people caring for someone with a disability who is not a spouse, partner or child under eighteen.

Benefits available for those on low income

Tenants on very low income, except for students, will usually be able to claim council tax benefit. This can cover up to 100% of the council tax. Tenants with disabilities may be entitled to further discounts. Tenants who are not responsible for individual council tax, but pay it through their rent, can claim housing benefit to cover the increase. The rules covering council tax liability can be obtained from a Citizens Advice Bureau or from your local authority council tax department.

Service charges
What is a service charge?

A service charge covers provision of services other than those covered by the rent.

A rental payment will normally cover maintenance charges, loan charges if any, and also profit. Other services, such as cleaning and gardening, will be covered by a separate charge, known as a service charge. A *registered* rent reflects the cost of any services provided by the landlord. An assured rent set by a landlord will normally include services, which must be outlined in the agreement.

The fact that the charges are variable must be written into a tenancy agreement and the landlord has a legal duty to provide the tenant with annual budgets and accounts and has to consult when he or she wishes to spend over a certain amount of money, currently £250 per dwelling..

The form of consultation, which must take place, is that of writing to all those affected and informing them of:

1. The landlord's intention to carry out work; this letter must give four weeks notice and a chance to feedback with objections or otherwise. Also the letter must outline Why these works are seen to be necessary;
2. The estimated cost of the works; At least two estimates or the inviting of them to see two estimates.

A period of twenty-eight days must be allowed before work is carried out. This gives time for any feedback from tenants.

The landlord can incur reasonable expense, without consultation, if the work is deemed to be necessary, i.e. emergency works.

If a service charge is variable then a landlord has certain legal obligations, which are clearly laid out in the 1985 and 1987 Landlord and Tenant Acts, as amended by the 1996 Housing Act and the 2002 Commonhold and Leasehold Reform Act.

Deposits
Tenancy Deposit Protection Scheme
The Tenancy Deposit Protection Scheme was introduced to protect all deposits paid to landlords after 6th April 2007. After this date, landlords and/or agents must use a government authorised scheme to protect deposits. The need for such a scheme has arisen because of the historical problem with deposits and the abuse of deposits by landlords.

The scheme works as follows:

Moving into a property

At the beginning of a new tenancy agreement, the tenant will pay a deposit to the landlord or agent as usual. Within 14 days the landlord is required to give the tenant details of how the deposit is going to be protected including:

- the contact details of the tenancy deposit scheme
- the contact details of landlord or agent
- how to apply for the release of the deposit
- what to do if there is a dispute about the deposit

There are three tenancy deposit schemes that your landlord can opt for:

Tenancy Deposit Solutions Ltd
www.mydeosits.co.uk
info@mydeposits.co.uk

The Tenancy Deposit Scheme
www.tds.gb.com
0845 226 7837

The Deposit Protection Service
www.depositprotection.com
0870 707 1 707

The schemes above fall into two categories, insurance based schemes and custodial schemes.

Custodial Scheme

- The tenant pays the deposit to the landlord
- The landlord pays the deposit into the scheme

- Within 14 days of receiving the deposit, the landlord must give the tenant prescribed information
- A the end of the tenancy, if the landlord and tenant have agreed how much of the deposit is to be returned, they will tell the scheme which returns the deposit, divided in the way agreed by the parties.
- If there is a dispute, the scheme will hold the disputed amount until the dispute resolution service or courts decide what is fair
- The interest accrued by deposits in the scheme will be used to pay for the running of the scheme and any surplus will be used to offer interest to the tenant, or landlord if the tenant isn't entitled to it.

Insurance based schemes
- The tenant pays the deposit to the landlord
- The landlord retains the deposit and pays a premium to the insurer (this is the key difference between the two schemes)
- Within 14 days of receiving a deposit the landlord must give the tenant prescribed information.
- At the end of the tenancy if the landlord and tenant agree how the deposit is to be divided or otherwise then the landlord will return the amount agreed
- If there is a dispute, the landlord must hand over the disputed amount to the scheme for safekeeping until the dispute is resolved
- If for any reason the landlord fails to comply, the insurance arrangements will ensure the return of the deposit to the tenant if they are entitled to it.

If your landlord or agent hasn't protected your deposit with one of the above then you can apply to your local county court for an order for the landlord either to protect the deposit or repay it.

The right to quiet enjoyment of a home
Earlier, we saw that when a tenancy agreement is signed, the landlord is contracting to give quiet enjoyment of the tenants home. This means that they have the right to live peacefully in the home without harassment.

The landlord is obliged not to do anything that will disturb the right to the quiet enjoyment of the home. The most serious breach of this right would be for the landlord to wrongfully evict a tenant.

Eviction: what can be done against unlawful harassment and eviction

It is a criminal offence for a landlord unlawfully to evict a residential occupier (whether or not a tenant!). The occupier has protection under the Protection from Eviction Act 1977 section 1(2). If the tenant or occupier is unlawfully evicted his/her first course should be to seek an injunction compelling the landlord to readmit him/her to the premises. *It is an unfortunate fact but many landlords will attempt to evict tenants forcefully. In doing so they break the law.* However, the landlord may, on termination of the tenancy recover possession without a court order if the agreement was entered into after 15th January 1989 and it falls into one of the following six situations:

The occupier shares any accommodation with the landlord and the landlord occupies the premises as his or her only or principal home.

The occupier shares any of the accommodation with a member of the landlords family, that person occupies the premises as their only or principal home, and the landlord occupies as his or her only or principal home premises in the same building.

The tenancy or licence was granted temporarily to an occupier who entered the premises as a trespasser.

The tenancy or licence gives the right to occupy for the purposes of a holiday.

The tenancy or licence is rent-free.

The licence relates to occupation of a hostel.

There is also a section in the 1977 Protection from Eviction Act which provides a defense for otherwise unlawful eviction and that is that the landlord may repossess if it is thought that the tenant no longer lives on the premises. It is important to note that, in order for such action to be seen as a crime under the 1977 Protection from Eviction Act, the intention of the landlord to evict must be proved.

However, there is another offence, namely harassment, which also needs to be proved. Even if the landlord is not guilty of permanently depriving a tenant of their home he/she could be guilty of harassment.

Such actions as cutting off services, deliberately allowing the premises to fall into a state of disrepair, or even forcing unwanted sexual attentions, all constitute harassment and a breach of the right to *quiet enjoyment*.

The 1977 Protection from Eviction Act also prohibits the use of violence to gain entry to premises. Even in situations where the landlord has the right to gain entry without a court order it is an offence to use violence.

If entry to the premises is opposed then the landlord should gain a court order

What can be done against unlawful evictions?
There are two main remedies for unlawful eviction: damages and, as stated above, an injunction.

The injunction
An injunction is an order from the court requiring a person to do, or not to do something. In the case of eviction the court can grant an injunction requiring the landlord to allow a tenant back into occupation of the premises. In the case of harassment an order can be made preventing the landlord from harassing the tenant.

Failure to comply with an injunction is contempt of court and can result in a fine or imprisonment.

Damages
In some cases the tenant can press for *financial compensation* following unlawful eviction. Financial compensation may have to be paid in cases

where financial loss has occurred or in cases where personal hardship alone has occurred.

The tenant can also press for *special damages,* which means that the tenant may recover the definable out-of-pocket expenses. These could be expenses arising as a result of having to stay in a hotel because of the eviction. Receipts must be kept in that case. There are also *general damages,* which can be awarded in compensation for stress, suffering and inconvenience.

A tenant may also seek *exemplary damages* where it can be proved that the landlord has disregarded the law deliberately with the intention of making a profit out of the displacement of the tenant.

Repairs and improvements

Repairs are essential works to keep the property in good order. Improvements are alterations to the property, e.g. the installation of a shower.

As we have seen, most tenancies are periodic, i.e. week-to-week or month-to-month. If a tenancy falls into this category, or is a fixed-term tenancy for less than seven years, and began after October1961, then a landlord is legally responsible for most major repairs to the flat or house.

If a tenancy began after 15th January 1989 then, in addition to the above responsibility, the landlord is also responsible for repairs to common parts and service fittings.

The area of law dealing with the landlord and tenants repairing obligations is the 1985 Landlord and Tenant Act, section 11.

This section of the Act is known as a covenant and cannot be excluded by informal agreement between landlord and tenant. In other words the landlord is legally responsible whether he or she likes it or not. Parties to a tenancy, however, may make an application to a court mutually to vary or exclude this section.

An example of repairs a landlord is responsible for:

Leaking roofs and guttering;
Rotting windows;

145

Rising damp;
Damp walls;
Faulty electrical wiring;
Dangerous ceilings and staircases;
Faulty gas and water pipes;
Broken water heaters and boilers;
Broken lavatories, sinks or baths.

In shared housing the landlord must see that shared halls, stairways, kitchens and bathrooms are maintained and kept clean and lit.

Normally, tenants are responsible only for minor repairs, e.g., broken door handles, cupboard doors, etc. Tenants will also be responsible for decorations unless they have been damaged as a result of the landlord's failure to do repair.

A landlord will be responsible for repairs only if the repair has been reported. It is therefore important to report repairs in writing and keep a copy. If the repair is not carried out then action can be taken. Damages can also be claimed.

Compensation can be claimed, with the appropriate amount being the reduction in the value of the premises to the tenant caused by the landlord's failure to repair. If the tenant carries out the repairs then the amount expended will represent the decrease in value.

The tenant does not have the right to withhold rent because of a breach of repairing covenant by the landlord. However, depending on the repair, the landlord will not have a very strong case in court if rent is withheld.

Reporting repairs to a landlord
The tenant has to tell the landlord or the person collecting the rent straight away when a repair needs doing. It is advisable that it is in writing, listing the repairs that need to be done.

Once a tenant has reported a repair the landlord must do it within a reasonable period of time. What is reasonable will depend on the nature of the repair. If certain emergency work needs to be done by the council, such as leaking guttering or drains a notice can be served ordering the landlord to do the work within a short time. In exceptional cases if a home cannot be made habitable at reasonable cost the council may declare that the house must no longer be used, in which case the council has a legal duty to rehouse a tenant.

If after the council has served notice the landlord still does not do the work, the council can send in its own builder or, in some cases take the landlord to court. A tenant must allow a landlord access to do repairs. The landlord has to give twenty-four hours notice of wishing to gain access.

The tenants rights whilst repairs are being carried out

The landlord must ensure that the repairs are done in an orderly and efficient way with minimum inconvenience to the tenant If the works are disruptive or if property or decorations are damaged the tenant can apply to the court for compensation or, if necessary, for an order to make the landlord behave reasonably.

If the landlord genuinely needs the house empty to do the work he/she can ask the tenant to vacate it and can if necessary get a court order against the tenant.

A *written agreement* should be drawn up making it clear that the tenant can move back in when the repairs are completed and stating what the arrangements for fuel charges and rent are.

If a person is an *assured* tenant the landlord could get a court order to make that person give up the home permanently if there is work to be done with him/her in occupation in occupation.

Can the landlord put the rent up after doing repairs?

If there is a service charge for maintenance, the landlord may be able to pass on the cost of the work(s).

Tenants rights to make improvements to a property

Unlike carrying out repairs the tenant will not normally have the right to insist that the landlord make actual alterations to the home. However, a tenant needs the following amenities and the law states that you should have them:

Bath or shower;

Wash hand basin;
Hot and cold water at each bath, basin or shower;
An indoor toilet.

If these amenities do not exist then the tenant can contact the council's Environmental Health Officer. An improvement notice can be served on the landlord ordering him to put the amenity in.

Disabled tenants

If a tenant is disabled he/she may need special items of equipment in the accommodation. The local authority may help in providing and, occasionally, paying for these. The tenant will need to obtain the permission of the landlord. If you require more information then contact the social services department locally.

Shared housing. The position of tenants in shared houses (Houses in Multiple Occupation)

The law lays down special standards for shared housing (houses in multiple occupation). These are usually bedsit houses of more than four people. Local authorities have special powers to deal with bad conditions when they occur. The legal regulations for houses in multiple occupation are set out in the Housing (Management of Houses in Multiple Occupation) Regulations 1990 and also the Housing Act 1996. The Housing Act 2004 has also introduced a system of licensing for houses in multi-occupation which are defined as a property with more than three flats with unrelated occupants. Any landlord managing such a property will be required to obtain a license from the LA. This took effect in April 2006. For further details you should contact your local authority.

The manager of a house in multiple occupation has responsibilities under the management regulations to carry out repair, maintenance and cleaning work and also safety work necessary to protect residents from risk of injury. A notice must be displayed where all the residents can see it showing the name, address and telephone number of the manager. Landlords must ensure that main entrances shared passageways, staircases and other common areas are maintained. All services such as gas, electricity and water supplies, plus drainage facilities, must also be maintained.

The same rules apply to the internal areas of living accommodation. In addition, there is a duty to maintain adequate fire safety, as obviously, shared housing is at greater risk of fire. Self-closing fire doors, emergency escape lighting, fire alarms and detectors and fire fighting equipment will normally be required. Signs indicating fire escape routes must be displayed where they are easy to see.

There are also rules concerning overcrowding in shared housing. The local authority has powers to tackle overcrowding problems; landlords, on request, have to supply the local authority with numbers of individuals and households in a shared house. Tenants also have duties, which enable landlords to fulfill their legal responsibilities. Tenants should allow landlords access at reasonable times, give details of all who live in the accommodation, and take care to avoid damage to property.

Sanitation health and hygiene

Local authorities have a duty to serve an owner with a notice requiring the provision of WCs when a property has insufficient sanitation, sanitation meaning toilet waste disposal. They will also serve notice if it is thought that the existing sanitation is inadequate and is harmful to health or is a nuisance. Local authorities have similar powers under various Public Health Acts to require owners to put right bad drains and sewers, also food storage facilities and vermin, plus the containing of disease.

The Environmental Health Department, if it considers the problem bad enough will serve a notice requiring the landlord to put the defect right. In certain cases the local authority can actually do the work and require the landlord to pay for it. This is called work *in default*.

Going to court to regain possession of a home

There may come a time when you need to go to court to regain possession of your property. This will usually arise when the contract has been breached by the tenant, for non-payment of rent or for some other breach such as nuisance or harassment.

149

As we have seen, a tenancy can be brought to an end in a court on one of the grounds for possession. However, as the tenancy will usually be an assured shorthold then it is necessary to consider whether you are in a position to give two months notice and withhold the deposit, as opposed to going to court.

If you decide, for whatever reason, to go to court, then any move to regain your property for breach of agreement will commence in the county court in the area in which the property is. The first steps in ending the tenancy will necessitate the serving of a notice of seeking possession using one of the Grounds for Possession detailed earlier in the book. If the tenancy is protected then 28 days must be given, the notice must be in prescribed form and served on the tenant personally (preferably).

If the tenancy is assured shorthold, which is more often the case now, then 14 days notice of seeking possession can be used. In all cases the ground to be relied upon must be clearly outlined in the notice.

If the case is more complex, then this will entail a particulars of claim being prepared, usually by a solicitor, as opposed to a standard possession form.

A fee is paid when sending the particulars and summons to court, which is currently £150. Both of these forms can be obtained from the court. When completed, the forms should be sent in duplicate to the county court and a copy retained for you.

The court will send a copy of the Particulars of claim and the summons to the tenant. They will send you a form which gives you a case number and court date to appear, known as the return date.

On the return date, you should arrive at court at least 15 minutes early. You can represent yourself in simple cases but are advised to use a solicitor for more contentious cases.

When it is your turn to present the case, you should have your file in order, a copy of all relevant notices served and a current rent arrears figure or a copy of the particulars for other cases. If it is simple rent arrears then quite often the judge will guide you through. However, the following are the steps to observe:

State your name and address
Tenants name and address

Start date of tenancy
Current rent and arrears
Date notice served-a copy should be produced for the judge
Circumstances of tenant (financial and other) this is where you make
Your case
Copy of order wanted

If the tenant is present then they will have a chance to defend themselves.

A number of orders are available. However, if you have gone to court on the mandatory ground eight then if the fact is proved then you will get possession immediately. If not, then the judge can grant an order, suspended whilst the tenant finds time to pay.

In a lot of cases, it is more expedient for a landlord to serve notice-requiring possession, if the tenancy has reached the end of the period, and then wait two months before the property is regained. This saves the cost and time of going to court particularly if the ground is one of nuisance or other, which will involve solicitors.

In many cases, if you are contemplating going to court and have never been before and do not know the procedure then it is best to use a solicitor to guide the case through. Costs can be recovered from the tenant, although this depends on the tenant's means.

If you regain possession of your property midway through the contractual term then you will have to complete the possession process by use of bailiff, a fee of £120 and another form, Warrant for Possession of Land used.

If you have reached the end of the contractual term and wish to recover your property then a "fast track" procedure is available which entails gaining an order for possession and bailiff's order by post. This can be used in cases with the exception of rent arrears.

14

THE POLICE – GETTING ARRESTED – HOW TO MAKE A COMPLAINT AGAINST THE POLICE

There are many reasons why the police might arrest a citizen, a few of those are:

- Driving offences
- Burglary
- Carrying offensive weapons
- Fighting
- Drink and drugs

If the police suspect that you are carrying offensive weapons or other illegal items or substances, they can stop and search without a warrant. If this happens then you can ask to see identification and you have the right to ask why you are being stopped and searched. The police do not have the right to intimidate or bully you.

Search of premises or home
The police have powers to search a premises or a home if they feel that evidence against you found there can help them with their enquiries. They can search a premise's with the consent of an occupier, or a warrant can be obtained from a magistrate to further their enquiries. They can search any premises without a warrant on a number of occasions such as:

- To capture an escaped prisoner
- To protect life or to stop serious damage to property

- Arrest someone for an arrestable offence or public disorder offence
- After an arrest to search a detained persons premises

Many other laws give police powers to enter premises, i.e. terrorism, harbouring an escaped convict and so on. Someone is allowed to be present when the search is taking place unless they might hinder the investigation. The police should give information about their powers to search premises. They are not allowed to use unreasonable force and a record must be kept of the search..

You have no legal obligation or duty to help the police with their enquiries. The only way the police can force you to accompany them to the police station is to arrest you. The police can arrest a suspect by obtaining an arrest warrant from a magistrate. The magistrate will need to be convinced that there is a case against a suspect. Police also have powers of arrest without a warrant in the following circumstances:

- An arrestable offence (one carrying a potential five-year sentence) has or could have been committed
- Certain other specific offences have been committed such as rape, car theft, shoplifting or other theft offences
- If you are drunk or fail a breath test
- If you are soliciting or living off immoral earnings
- If you refuse to give details of your name and address if a particular law requires you to do so
- Where a breach of the peace has occurred or may occur.

What to do if you are arrested
It may be possible to avoid being arrested if you co-operate with the police in the first instance. However, if you are arrested, then you should be informed of your right to see a solicitor. It does not matter what time you are arrested, the duty solicitor scheme will mean that a solicitor will be on call and will speak to you over the telephone or come out to see you.

You should also be told that you have the right to inform some other person of your arrest. You should be told that you have a right to see the codes of practice followed by the police. You should be given a written note of the three rights above, which will contain the usual caution: '*You do not have to say anything, but it may harm your defence if you do not mention when questioned something which you later rely on in court. Anything you do say may be given in evidence*'.

This caution means that you have the right of silence. You do not have to say anything, in particular until a solicitor arrives. In very limited cases, the right of silence has been removed. What you say can be used in any legal proceedings that are brought against you.

It is generally wise to say nothing until a solicitor arrives and then the interview can be guided professionally. What you do say is tape-recorded.

Detaining suspects

If you have not been arrested then the police cannot keep you at the police station. When you have been arrested you should be charged with an offence within 24 hours (usually) or released. You can be held up to 36 hours for a serious offence. If the police wish to detain you for longer than this then they can apply to a magistrate's court for permission to do so. 72 hours is usually the maximum amount of time. The Police and Criminal Evidence Act (PACE) deals with rights when arrested.

Assuming that you have been charged with an offence then you will already have seen a solicitor. If you have not seen a solicitor then it is very wise to do so as they can guide you through the procedure and ensure that what takes place is fair.

After you have been charged, you will either be remanded in custody or let out on bail. If you are remanded in custody you will not be released until after the trial. Bail applications are not, or should not, be refused unnecessarily. However, you may have to provide sureties and comply with certain conditions such as reporting to the police station.

More minor offences are tried in the magistrate's court and more serious offences in the Crown Court. (See previous chapters).

You will need to prepare your case with your solicitor for the trial. There may be witnesses to locate and also statements to prepare. At the trial, you will either be found guilty or not guilty. If you are found not guilty there may be grounds for you to bring proceedings against the police for false imprisonment arising from your original arrest. If you are found guilty then you will be sentenced and at this stage any previous convictions are brought to light.

Once you have been convicted, you will have a criminal record. Some offences are so minor and commonplace that they are unlikely to affect your future employment or well being generally. However, more serious offences can have a serious effect and you should certainly take professional advice. Criminal records arising from different types of crime will last for different periods of time.

Making a complaint against the police

The Independent Police Complaints Authority (PTA) supervises investigations into complaints against the police. As a member of the public, you can make complaints about the conduct of a police officer towards yourself if you think that you have good reason. You can also complain on someone else's behalf if you have their written authorisation.

The Police Complaints Authority is an independent body set up by the government to oversee public complaints against police officers in the 43 police services in England and Wales, plus the British Transport Police, Ministry of Defence, Port of Liverpool, Port of Tilbury, Royal parks and UKAEA police. The PCA can investigate complaints direct from the public or referred directly from the police services.

If you do decide to make your complaint through the PCA, send the details to the following address, making sure that all the relevant information is included:

Police Complaints Authority
10 Great George Street London SW1P 3AE.
General enquiries tel: 020 7273 6450.
Alternatively, go to www.police complaints
You will access the website here and can get further in depth information relating to number and types of complaints and also further guidance.

Useful Addresses

The Legal system

The Court Service Secretariat
The Lord Chancellors Department
Southside
105 Victoria Street
London SW1E 6QT
020 7210 2059

Crown Prosecution Service
50 Ludgate Hill
London EC4M 7EX
020 7273 8152

The Free Representation Unit
49-51 Bedford Row
London WC1R 4LR
020 7 831 0692

The Institute of Legal Executives
Kempston Manor Kempston
Bedford MK42 7AB
01234 841000

The Law Society
113 Chancery Lane
London WC2A 1PL
020 7 242 1222

Legal Action Group
242 Pentonville Road
London N1 9UN
020 7833 8931

National Association of Citizens Advice bureau
115-123 Pentonville Road
London N1 9LZ
020 7833 2181

Solicitors Complaints Bureau
Portland House
Stag Place
London SW1E 5BL

Law and the Consumer

Advertising Standards Authority
Brook House
2-16 Torrington Place
London WC1E 7HN
020 7580 5555

Association of British Travel Agents
55-57 Newman Street
London W1P 4AH
0207 637 244

Consumers Association
2 Marylebone Road
London NW1 4DF
020 7486 544

Consumer Credit Association (UK)
Queens House
Queens Road
Chester CH1 3BQ
01244 312044

Direct Marketing Association
Haymarket House
1 Oxendon Street
London SW1Y 4EE
020 7321 2525

Direct Selling Association
29 Floral Street
London WC2E 9DP
020 7497 1234

Office of Fair Trading
Field House
15-25 Breame Buildings
London EC4 1PR
020 7242 2858

Employment Law

Advisory, Conciliation and Arbitration Service (ACAS)
27 Wilton Street
London SW1X 7AZ
020 7 210 3000

Commissioner for the Rights of Trade Union Members
First Floor
Bank Chambers
2A Rylands Street
Warrington
Cheshire WA1 1EN
01925 41571

Employment Appeal Tribunal
Audit House
Victoria Embankment

London EC4T ODS
020 7 273 1041

Health and Safety Executive
Broad Land
Sheffield
S3 7HQ
01742 892345

Children and the Law

Childline
2nd Floor
Royal Mail Building
Studd Street
London N1 OQW
020 7 239 1000

Child Support Agency
PO Box 55
Brierley Hill
West Midlands DY5 1YL
0345 133133

The Children's Society
Edward Rudolf House
Margery Street
London WC1X OJL
020 7 837 4299

Divorce

Relate Marriage Guidance
Herbert Gray College

Little Church Street
Rugby
Warwickshire CV21 3AP
0788 573241

The Information Office
National Council for one Parent Families
255 Kentish Town Road
London NW5 2LX

Bereavement

Age Concern
England
Astral House 1268 London Road
Norbury
London SW16 4ER
Tel: 0181 679 8000
Fax: 0181 679 6069

Age Concern Funeral Plan
Tel 0800 387735 (freephone)
0181 765 7233 (general enquiry's)

Asian Funeral Service
209 Kenton road
Harrow
Middlesex HA3 OHD
Tel: 0181 909 3737

Association of Burial Authorities
139 Kensington High Street
London W8 6SU
Tel: 0171 937 0052
Fax: 0171 937 1393

British Organ Donors Society (Body)
Balsham,
Cambridge CB1 6DL
Tel/Fax 01223 893636

Cremation Society
2nd Floor, Brecon House
16-16a Albion Place
Maidstone ME14 5DZ
Tel: 01622 688292/3
Fax: 01622 686698

Cruse-Bereavement Care
Cruse House, 126 Sheen Road
Richmond, TW9 1UR
Tel: 0181 940 4818
Fax: 0181 940 7638

Foundation for the Study of Infant Death
14 Halkin Street
London SW1X 7DP
Tel: 0171 235 0965

In addition to the above addresses there is useful information available on the internet. This is usually accessed by entering the main key words, i.e. for divorce www.divorce.

For more in depth information on each of the individual areas, go to our web-site www. Straightforwardco.co.uk where you can purchase books direct, such as Employment Law, Consumer Law, Divorce and The Law, Family Law, Bereavement and the Law, Producing a will, Landlord and Tenant etc. A complete list is available by directly printing a catalogue from our site or e- mailing us at: Info@straightforwardco.co.uk.

www.straightforwardco.co.uk

All titles, listed below, in the Straightforward Guides Series can be purchased online, using credit card or other forms of payment by going to www.straightfowardco.co.uk A discount of 25% per title is offered with online purchases.

Law
A Straightforward Guide to:
Consumer Rights
Bankruptcy Insolvency and the Law
Employment Law
Private Tenants Rights
Family law
Small Claims in the County Court
Contract law
Intellectual Property and the law
Divorce and the law
Leaseholders Rights
The Process of Conveyancing
Knowing Your Rights and Using the Courts
Producing Your own Will
Housing Rights
The Bailiff the law and You
Probate and The Law
Company law
What to Expect When You Go to Court
Guide to Competition Law
Give me Your Money-Guide to Effective Debt Collection
Caring for a Disabled Child

General titles
Letting Property for Profit
Buying, Selling and Renting property
Buying a Home in England and France
Bookkeeping and Accounts for Small Business

Creative Writing
Freelance Writing
Writing Your own Life Story
Writing performance Poetry
Writing Romantic Fiction
Speech Writing

Teaching Your Child to Read and write
Teaching Your Child to Swim
Raising a Child-The Early Years

Creating a Successful Commercial Website
The Straightforward Business Plan
The Straightforward C.V.
Successful Public Speaking

Handling Bereavement
Play the Game-A Compendium of Rules
Individual and Personal Finance
Understanding Mental Illness
The Two Minute Message
Guide to Self Defence
Buying a Used Car
Tiling for Beginners

Go to:
www.straightforwardco.co.uk